THE
MAKING
OF A MAN

WHAT A **WOMAN WANTS** AND A **MAN NEEDS**

T0167413

BART **MALONE**
DR. HENRY **MALONE**

THE
MAKING
OF A MAN

WHAT A **WOMAN WANTS**
AND A **MAN NEEDS**

Distributed by:
Bart Malone Ministries
273 Bellagio Circle,
Sandford Florida 32771 USA

www.BARTMALONE.com

Book Layout and Cover Design by *Alison Miller*
www.MHArtwork.net

Printed in the United States of America

TABLE OF **CONTENTS**

Foreword

Bart Malone in his book, The Making of a Man, What a Woman Wants and a Man Needs, with bold transparency, and clear forthrightness presents the need for masculinity and femininity in a world that is quickly trying to neuter men and to keep young boys from desiring manhood. It is also trying to masculinize women, and toughen them to the point that the life of the child within them is simply a piece of flesh that until birth does not become human. Metrosexual is increasingly touted by the media, and the strength of being as masculine as God made man to be is objected to as being brutish and boring and historical femininity is distained as weak and benign. I am encouraged by the way Bart challenges that line of thinking.

From the very beginning man and woman have been very different from each other. However, the term "different" does not make one or the other more valuable. God does nothing by happenstance or chance. He created man outside the garden and He made woman inside the Garden. That fact gives insight that God, with great intention, made them to be more than anatomically different from the beginning.

With His order of creation God made a statement about masculinity and femininity. With His creation of anatomical differences He gave them ability to become one as both give and receive. From that oneness He gave them the ability to be fruitful, and from the fruit of their children He gave them the ability to multiply as their children then bear fruit of their own. In each way, God gives the man and the woman the means to make the Earth better.

God then placed man inside the Garden and gave Man clear instructions concerning the rules of the Garden. He also gave man a taste for the wild and untamed so the Garden would grow, and gave woman a taste for the tamed and stable so the Garden would flourish and produce food. God made man to conquer, and to protect outside the garden, and woman to do the same inside it. While this realization has various blends of intensity and passion within each man or woman it, as a whole, has proven true.

Man and woman are to be alike in so many ways. They are to be tender, kind, gentle, loving, romantic, courageous, visionary and envisioning of others; but they express this sameness in far different ways. It is the blend of the sameness and it is the evidence of their differentness that strengthens the family. It is the stuff that allows sons to become masculine and daughters to become feminine. It forms a boy in his youth to become a great husband and father. It shapes a girl to become a great wife and mother. In turn their children become like them.

Bart gives insight and wisdom in exposing the problems we create when we get those roles crossed. When sex becomes a means of self-gratification rather than an expression of love, marriages will become a convenience rather than a covenant. Sadly, every convenience can quickly turn into an inconvenience and divorce becomes the evidence of love turned selfish.

Bart covers a wide swath of topics and one cannot read this book without stopping to think that it would have been good to know these things much earlier that we now do. Yet, we should not forget, God is a transforming God and none of us are too old to be transformed.

John Paul Jackson
Founder and Chairman
Streams Ministries International
John Paul Jackson Ministries

Chapter 1
Find Your Face, Discover Your Place

Finding manhood or womanhood are requirements for 'finding your face' (learning who you are) and 'discovering your place' (understanding your purpose).

Who are you? Why are you here? Everyone seeks to define themselves. Those, whose worldview does not include a Creator God, see themselves as a mere accident of evolution and their lives as whatever they make of them. Like the atheists, those who do not believe in a *personal* God and have not found their Savior, are also doomed to failure in their search for meaning. To find the 'meaning of life,' you must discover — who's your daddy?

In the Beginning
To get a grip on who you are, and where you are going, you first have to figure out how you came to be here. No one, regardless of the circumstances of their conception, is merely the result of a chance combination of their parents' DNA. God was directly and personally involved in our formation, and He placed within each of us the potential to become one-of-a-kind winners. David explains this mystery in Psalms 139:13-16:

> *You made all the delicate, inner parts of my body and knit me together in my mother's womb. Thank you for making me so*

wonderfully complex! Your workmanship is marvelous — and how well I know it. You watched me as I was being formed in utter seclusion, as I was woven together in the dark of the womb. You saw me before I was born. Every day of my life was recorded in your book. Every moment was laid out before a single day had passed (NLT).

Yes, even before *you* were born, God knew you, and He took the materials your parents donated and combined them to form YOU — a unique individual — a person with a destiny and important purpose. God told the "Weeping Prophet" in Jeremiah 1:4:

"... I knew you before I formed you in your mother's womb. Before you were born I set you apart and appointed you as my spokesman to the world" (NLT).

God is not just *a* father ... He's *your* father.

Reason for Being

Why would God go to the effort to make us if He did not have a purpose for our existence? The knowledge that each one has a purpose is buried within every person. God created everyone *on purpose, for a purpose*. Ephesians 2:10, confirms this:

For we are His workmanship, created in Christ Jesus for good works, which God prepared beforehand that we should walk in them (NKJV).

When we *really* believe we have a purpose, and that God *really* will assist us in fulfilling it, our faith is empowered with a courage that will cause us to become the person God intended. However, some may look at their human ancestry and fail to see the hand of God. Others may look at their past mistakes and missed opportunities, and think that there is little hope that anything good can come of their lives.

When the master sculptor, Michelangelo, created the remarkable statue "David," he did not search the world over for a piece of rock that looked like the figure he wanted to create. No, he drew forth something great from an ordinary piece of marble (actually a stone that had been rejected by other sculptors). And, that is exactly what God wants to do with each of us. He wants to draw forth that which He instilled within us. Once we come into the world, God uses the circumstances of life, similar to the way a sculptor uses his tools, to fashion us into the person He intends us to be. Nevertheless, to become all God planned, we must actively participate with Him in that 'shaping' process.

You can know that God created you and be aware that He has a purpose for your life but you will never be who you *are* or fulfill your *purpose* until you become routed in the fatherhood of God and rediscover your 'image.'

Shattered Likeness

Have you ever looked in the mirror and wondered who was staring back at you?

Perhaps you remember learning that man was created in the image of God:
> *So God created man in His own image; in the image of God*
> *He created him; male and female He created them* (Genesis
> 1:27 NKJV).

Obviously, man was not created in the physical likeness of God, who the Bible teaches is a spirit. Yet, Adam's body mirrored the life found in God because it was perfectly healthy and eternal. However, the 'image of God' refers primarily to the imprint of God's prototype upon the human spirit, mind, will, and emotions. This 'likeness' enabled Adam and Eve to know what God meant for them to be as male person and female person and to understand their gender-related functions — morally and socially — in God's creation.

Like God, the first couple had the capacity to make free-will choices. Although they were given a 'righteous' nature, they made an evil choice and rebelled against their Creator. This decision was disastrous for them and for us. It marred their 'image' and damaged God's likeness within all their descendants:
> *Therefore, just as through one man sin entered the world,*
> *and death through sin, and thus death spread to all men,*
> *because all sinned* (Romans 5:12 NKJV).

The Good News is that when Jesus took upon Himself the sins of the world, He redeemed mankind, and those who receive Him as Savior are restored to relationship with God and re-established to His 'likeness.' Although a person's spirit is *immediately* restored to the 'likeness of God' at salvation, the restoration of the mind, will, emotions, and body is a process: *"Put on your new nature, created to be **like God**—truly righteous and holy"* (Ephesians 4:24 NLT, emphasis added). Becoming established in manhood and womanhood is putting on the new masculine and feminine nature that is necessary to become all we were created to be.

My Roommate, Mr. Pete

(Henry recalls) When Mr. Pete became a born-again Christian, he lost everything. After burning his Bible and making his life hell on earth for months, his family discovered that he would not give up his new beliefs. So, his wife and other family members, who were followers of another Christian faith, threw him out with only a few of his things in a tin suitcase, and told him to never return.

My father saw Mr. Pete, with his tin suitcase, and when my Dad learned that he was homeless, Dad invited him to stay with us. This man, who had lost everything that he valued because of his stand for Christ, could easily have been angry with God and man, and disillusioned with life. Instead, this unlikely person became a model for manhood to me, his six-year old roommate. He taught me that being a man is living by a moral code that includes responsibility, integrity, honesty, and courage.

During the six years Mr. Pete stayed with us, and shared my bedroom, he also shared, by example, what Christian manhood looks like to a clueless little boy. During those six years, I learned from this simple, unassuming person that *real* men ...

- Keep their word even if it costs them much
- Maintain a gentle, quiet spirit when feeling frustrated or facing angry people
- Control their passions and keep their lives clean
- Keep short accounts with God by faithfully reading the Bible and praying everyday
- Live by a code of conduct that requires faithfulness, honesty, integrity, and courage

I learned from Mr. Pete that manhood is not a way of *acting* — being tough or macho — but a way of *being*. Real manhood must find a balance between two opposites, such as:

> Being a champion for truth — while also being merciful and full of grace
>
> Being a courageous hero — while also being sympathetic, humble, and approachable

The prophet Micah captured the heart of manhood when he wrote, by the Holy Spirit:

> *... What does the LORD require of you? To act justly and to love mercy and to walk humbly with your God* (Micah 6:8 NIV).

- "To act justly" means living and interacting with others by God's value system
- "To love mercy" refers to the attitude of being full or compassion toward others
- "To walk humbly with your God" speaks of being unpretentious in your faith and relationship with God.

Actually, a real man looks and acts like the ultimate model for manhood, Jesus. Although the Bible abounds with models for manhood, Jesus provides the only *perfect* model for how God intends man to operate on the earth. Jesus demonstrated the image, lifestyle, and values for which men were created.

Jesus showed self-control when confronted with temptation ... He was strong and courageous when dealing with those who opposed Him ... He walked in integrity at all times, and even while suffering the agony of crucifixion, He still took responsibility for His mother's future needs.

My Journey Into Manhood
I (Bart) was fortunate in many ways to have a father who understood about manhood and its importance. He used the occasion of my wedding to create a 'rite of passage' that called me into manhood.

There must come a time when a man breaks free of paternal and maternal bonds. It doesn't mean that he stops loving his parents, but that he no longer requires their approval to feel good about himself, and their permission or advice to make life's decisions. Although he may ask for their wisdom and counsel, he makes his own decisions, and follows his own destiny. In Luke 14: 26-27, Jesus explained it like this:

> If you want to be my disciple, you must hate everyone else by comparison—your father and mother, wife and children, brothers and sisters—yes, even your own life. Otherwise, you cannot be my disciple (NLT).

While growing up, I enjoyed doing masculine things like contact sports and other risk-taking endeavor. I moved away from Dallas (and my parents) when I was in my 30s after being married for eight years, having three children, starting a successful business, and being on my own for over a decade. That move was the final break in my *paternal* bond. My *maternal* bond was broken at 19-years-old, when I left home to explore the world. Thank God for wise women, like my mother, who hear from God and recognize when it is best to 'back off' and allow their sons to go their own way.

My father guided me as far as he could in the process of cultivating my manhood, then God provided a mentor who, unlike my more sympathetic father, would not cut me an ounce of slack. It was a tremendous privilege to have John Paul Jackson for a mentor, but it was also painful. I had many rough edges he chipped away at for most a decade.

As a classic overachiever, I craved the status of 'insider' and 'favorite son.' However, my integrity did not measure up to those ambitions, or to John Paul's high standards. So, his mission as my mentor was to help me grow in integrity, but he was never mean, vindictive, shaming, or manipulative. Yet, at the time, I felt that he was overly harsh because he never once allowed me to get off easy on a character issue. Consequently, John Paul gave me a lot of what I needed, constructive criticism and discipline, and very little of the things I craved, promotion and approval. I was 33-years-old when he fired me from his ministry over a misunderstanding.

When I returned to Dallas, the pain of what seemed like an unjust rejection, from a man I deeply respected, haunted me. (We later reconnected, he recognized his mistake, and I am presently the senior pastor of a church that is part of John Paul Jackson's Association of Bridge Churches. Again I have the benefit of his friendship, mentoring, and pastoral oversight.) But, when I moved home to Dallas, that lay many years in the future and was unimaginable.

Before leaving Texas to join John Paul's ministry, I had experienced a $40 million business failure. So, I was returning to a world that I felt had also rejected me, and I felt like a stranger in my hometown. I took over management of my father's ministry and immediately went to work helping him create a new business plan that would give it a needed face-lift. We leased new office space and laid the groundwork to begin a new church. Then, on the *very day* we were to re-launch his ministry, Dad came to my office and told me that he was taking a sabbatical, to deal with a personal issue.

From my standpoint, the timing could not have been worse. I felt like the pilot of a ship scheduled to leave port that was now tied indefinitely to the dock. That setback on top of everything else was too much for me to handle ... way too much! After a $40 million business failure, being mistakenly accused of wrong doing and fired by my mentor, this was the last straw! I was completely overwhelmed — at the end of my rope.

On that day, my need for approval from my father, John Paul, or anyone else died. I felt empty, isolated, and completely alone in the world. I felt betrayed by my father, my mentor, and even by my God. As I climbed into my vehicle to go home that day, I seemed that my world was crashing around me. As got on the highway to make the 45-minute commute home, I cried out to God in anguish. I told Him how very disappointed I was in Him and His management of the issues of my life. I shouted in despair, "What are You *doing* to me?"

At that moment, the sweet presence of the Holy Spirit filled my truck! His presence was so tangible; it was as though a physical person was in the passenger seat beside me. Tears began streaming down my face as He gently said; "Though your father and mother betray you, I will pick you up" (see Psalms 27:10). I pulled off the highway onto the shoulder of the road and sat hunched over the steering wheel. My heart pounded like a jack hammer in my chest, as I sobbed uncontrollably and those words echoed over and over through my mind. God was applying the healing potion of His love to my *wounded heart*.

In that powerful moment, I experienced *adoption*. The Lord fused His spirit to mine as He began healing the fragmented and wounded root of my masculinity, and connecting that root to Himself. Over the next few months, God recreated my manhood and dealt with various personal issues as He helped me walk through this most difficult period of my life.

Your journey discovering manhood will not be like mine. However, it will almost certainly have moments of difficulty, for you too must come to the end of your self-sufficiency. You must reach the place where you have nowhere left to turn before you can truly release yourself into the hands of God. Only then will you find your need for acceptance and approval completely and solely satisfied in Him. Then you can find your 'face' and your 'place,' and become the person capable of fulfilling you God-given purpose, the man God created you to be.

Action Steps
Please answer the following questions:
1. Do you feel that your Dad met *all* your fathering needs?
2. Did your mother provide *all* that you needed from her?
3. If you are a dad, have you successfully met *all* your children's needs?
4. Have you ever experienced a Rite of Passage ceremony during which you were 'called out' to join the company of men?
5. Do you believe that you have been adequately prepared to fulfill the purpose to which God destined you?

If, in all honesty, you must answer "No" to any of the foregoing questions, this book was written for you.

■■

In the next chapter ...
You will discover a truth about manhood that has nearly been lost, and find out why our society has misunderstood its importance.

Chapter 2
Manhood — What It Means to Be a Man

There is confusion about what 'manhood' is. Some in the American culture would like to redefine it to something more feminine. A 'politically correct' media depicts manhood in derogatory ways, as excessively sexual, violently aggressive or limp-wristed and gutless … and too many of our leaders are silent seemingly unaware that our culture is losing an important element of masculinity — the concept and experience of truly becoming a man.

Some look to our educational system to create men out of boys. However, most schools expect boys to act like girls, by requiring them to behave and learn in ways more suitable to females. Schools require children of both genders to sit quietly in rows without moving about and to listen to their instructor. This 'regimented style' may *seem* right because *we* were trained this way; however, it is not the best way for boys to learn. God fashioned them to be aggressors, warriors, and heroes. Most boys learn better from a hands-on approach. The attempt to force a square peg into a round hole can cause boys to feel alienated from the educational process, and to be labeled as "trouble makers," "unruly," and "hard to manage." An educational system that fails to recognize the fundamental differences in the learning styles of boys and girls certainly has no idea how to mold boys into men.

Women Only

Some moms try to help their sons move into manhood because, for one reason or another, the father does not take the lead. A mother may give her son added responsibility in an attempt to help him become manly. Unfortunately, these efforts do not help for the most part and can actually hinder the maturing process. Yes, boys do indeed need to learn to be responsible, but if that alone created manhood, then every young man who comes out of the military, or holds a job would be a man. Being 'responsible is a very important ingredient of adulthood for both men and women, but there is far more to becoming a man.

Manhood is often falsely attributed to boys when they attain a certain age (16, 18, or 21), and their first sexual encounter may be considered a 'rite of passage.' Manhood, however, is more than being old enough to get a driver's license, serve in the military, or buy liquor; and it is certainly much more than having sexual intercourse.

Fatherhood's Forgotten Function

It is time for men to break free from stereotypes to rediscover what God intended an adult male to be. Those who find *genuine* manhood will live in a power and blessing their less fortunate brothers cannot know because the pursuit of manhood makes men into champions.

God intends fathers to help their sons make the transition from childhood to manhood. Unfortunately, most fathers have no clue how to accomplish this because they themselves did not receive it. Ignoring manhood training has created generations of men with gaping *father wounds*. However, healing and restoration is within every man's reach.

Many of our fathers, and their fathers grew up influenced by beliefs developed during the "Victorian Age." This was at the beginning of the Industrial Revolution, when most men no longer engaged in a family craft or business and went outside the home for the first time to earn a living. Women, on the other hand, were expected to remain at home to raise the children. Because fathers retained little or no responsibility toward childrearing, generations of children grew up without their father's affection, blessing, or affirmation.

So-called experts of the day, advised men to leave childrearing to their wives who they claimed were "better equipped" for the job. Father became a remote 'pillar of strength' for the family with a distant relationship with his children. Consequently, most men grew up with aloof fathers who dysfunctional at home.

Women Only

It can be a big mistake for a single mom to tell her young son, "You are the man of the house." Placing a man's job on tiny shoulders can crush him and it hardly ever makes a boy become a man. In fact, this kind of announcement can produce both "Parental Inversion" and "Substitute Mates." The latter occurs when a boy takes on the role of a spouse to his mother, and relates to her as a husband would. This causes him to become co-dependent with her and, eventually, to rebel. The very thing that Mom hoped would help her son, and provide her comfort, may cause things to go terribly wrong in a number of ways. A boy without a father needs a male figure to give him guidance, supervision, and instruction in manhood (without excessive female intervention).

If the natural father is unavailable or incapable of raising your son, the Lord wants to provide a godly man to become the father figure he needs. Ask Him to provide such a person and discuss it with your pastor.

The Undiagnosed Disability — the Father Wound

Men who bear a *father wound* are often unaware of their problem, yet experience its symptoms. They may feel discontent with their lives or sense that something essential is missing. Some may have a sexual 'identity crisis.' Living with this undiagnosed, crippling disability causes many men to suffer needlessly from what is a curable condition.

Even those who had wonderful and godly fathers, I believe, received a *father wound*. (Please withhold judgment about whether you have it until you complete this entire chapter.) Unless a man allows God to heal him — which can only occur with his conscious awareness and participation — he will be among the walking wounded. Those who carry an injured spirit and soul are limited in their ability to succeed as men, husbands, fathers, and leaders. This wound not only makes reaching their God-intended potential impossible, it causes them to miss much of the joy of life and predestines their sons and daughters to be imprinted with the same wound. Those who might not seek healing of their *father wound* for themselves should do it for their children's sake.

A *father wound* results from having a human, imperfect father, who — regardless of his intentions and efforts — was unable to meet your needs. Unfortunately, most men who desire to be good dads have little understanding of how to follow through, and thus are destined to failure. New fathers are often immature, newly married, and still adjusting to having a wife. They are usually without training, experience, or a role model for raising children. Because our western lifestyle often has young fathers and mothers living independently and sometimes in a different city than their parents, the child-rearing wisdom of past generations is often a lost resource.

Some men may wonder how they could have a *father wound* without being aware of receiving it. Often, this wound is not caused by what their father's *did* but by what was left *undone*. Many men recognize that they missed 'something' from their fathers but may think of it only as a lack of attention or support. However, their loss often goes far deeper: they missed their father's mentoring into manhood.

Many men become accustomed to the way things are, and eventually decided that things can never be better. But, there is a higher level of living available to every man — an "abundant life" promised by Jesus in John 10:10.

If your father never experienced acceptance, validation, or mentoring into manhood from his dad, then he most likely could not give to you what you needed. Regardless of how hard he may have tried, your father could parent only as he was parented. As a father, you will more than likely do to your children exactly what was done to you. In this way, the sins of fathers are passed down to succeeding generations (Deuteronomy 5:9). However, the Lord is waiting for you to call upon Him to intervene, and to give you a paradigm shift — to "reverse the curse!"

WOMEN ONLY

Fathers wound both their sons and daughters. The healing of the male and female father wound is different for the most part but alike in some ways.

Once while I (Henry) was doing Personal Ministry Training, a man who was merely observing began to weep uncontrollably. This occurred during a deliverance session, so I quickly asked someone else to take charge. Then I began to work personally with this man, who needed to be pulled from the pain of deep rejection and abandonment. I discovered that his father had never loved and accepted him unconditionally, so he believed he had no "self-worth" and, in addition, had no sense of "belonging." Although there were women in the session with father wounds, they were not affected in the same way because their wounds were of a different nature.

After a lot of work, the man was able to forgive his father and release the wounds of his past. He experienced healing after an encounter with the Lord in which he came to understand that he was God's son and that he 'belonged' to Him. To find release from father wounds, each person, whether male or female, must come to understand that they are 'owned' by their heavenly Father. Women who carry father wounds can be just as dysfunctional with their children as men. They, too, should seek healing, for themselves, and so they will not imprint their woundedness upon their children.

Healing a *father wound* means much more than merely forgiving your dad for being a lousy father. Although, that is certainly a necessary step in finding release, this wound requires more than forgiveness. The *father wound* began in the Garden of Eden when Adam sinned and it continues through today. Adam was created in the image of God and when he fell, his self-image was broken. As his descendents, we inherited his brokenness which keeps us from adequately meeting the needs of our children. Most men and women stumble through life blind to their brokenness, but God has healing for everyone!

Dysfunctional Dads

The most fundamental concept of mentoring is that a person can only give to another what he himself possesses. Because the majority of fathers have little understanding of how to lead their sons into manhood, many boys grow up trying to emulate the dominating person in their life (which could be their mother), or they may copy media stereotypes, such as:

- John Wayne Dad — Uncommunicative, silent, standoffish, unaffectionate, a tough guy who never cries or show fear but is actually terrified to discuss *real* issues, express his *real* feelings, or go beyond superficial relationships
- Rambo Dad — A loner, perfectionist a man incapable of being satisfied, who believes that only he is the only one who can ever do a job exactly right. Whose answer to life's problems is to be a better physical specimen and fighter than others.
- Brainy Dad — The problem solver, who is unable to relate to his family on an emotional and personal level; who hides behind his mind and believes that a father's job is merely to solve his wife's and children's problems.
- The Invisible Dad — Missing from the home most of the time, the ghost dad is rarely 'there' for his wife and children because he is pursuing success or other interests. He may salve his guilt by being a great provider and meeting his family's financial needs and their desires and yet failing to provide what they really need — him.
- Macho Dad — An alienator who uses shame, intimidation, and threats of violence (strong discipline) to manipulate his family. Invariably a negative influence on his children, fear is all this dad has to give.

Was your father similar to any of these stereotypes, or a mixture of them?

But, more importantly, *who are you most like?* Regardless of how well, or poorly, your dad prepared you for manhood, I believe every man can be certain of two things:

1. You received a *father wound*
2. God wants to heal it.

Finding Your Feelings

Our culture encourages men to "get in touch with their feelings." Indeed, most men do need to do that; however, men will never process and express their emotions as women do. God created men to be different from women in many ways, and how they handle emotions is one of them.

Women Only

Some women may unconsciously wish to make their husbands into their 'best girl friend.' A man can be your best friend but he can never be like a girl friend that is knows how you feel because she feels the same way. Men do not live in the same emotional world that women inhabit. Men do not deal with emotions in the same time frame, use the same methods to process their feelings, or necessarily reach the same conclusions as women. A man wants to be far more than your girl friend — he wants to be your man! By giving up unrealistic expectations and allowing your guy to be who God intended, you will both enjoy a richer relationship.

Men, if you ignore your feelings and emotions, you encourage a state of denial and can place yourself into an abyss of numbness. You can experience a lack of feeling when your emotions are regularly ignored, and lose the ability to identify the circumstances that produce a given feeling.

I (Henry) have often ministered to men who have 'stuffed' their emotions so deeply they became lost. During a counseling session with one man, he told me how his wife had cheated on him and, with a cold and unemotional voice, he declared, "This does not affect me in any way ... I do not care." Knowing that he must admit to having feelings to forgive and find freedom, I got into his face and said with deep emotion, "This man was in *your* bed having sex with *your* wife — and YOU DID NOT CARE?" That touched his pain and his emotions erupted from hidden depths, and he screamed, "I could kill him!" The pain was there, but buried so deeply he could not touch it without great difficulty. It was lost to his conscious mind.

Feelings should be considered valuable tools by men because they inform us what is happening below the conscious level. Think of them as instruments in the cockpit of an airplane flying through a cloud. To avoid crashing, a man must watch and understand them. God designed our emotions to aid us in navigating our experiences and to enhance our enjoyment of life. Learning to harness and channel your emotions can significantly improve life. However, before men can use emotions for their good, many will need to first rediscover and value them as valid and important parts of manhood.

Women Only

Some well-meaning mothers may feel the need to make more, rather than less, input into a boy's life as he reaches 12 or 13 years of age. A boy entering his teens, however, wants to move toward manhood and needs the steady hand of a man to guide him through the ensuing difficult lessons.

At this stage, when a son asks questions, his mother for the most part, should refer him to his dad. Yes, you are capable of giving good answers and sound advice, but boys of this age need to learn from their fathers.

If his father is not in his life, then it is vital that you petition God to find a man willing to serve as a "father figure" to guide him along the path to manhood. In the culture of the Osage Indians, every man was responsible to help teach and guide his "sister-son" (his nephew) into manhood.

If a woman tries to make a man become woman-like in how he handles emotions, he will usually cling all the tighter to whatever model of manhood he knows. Most men in our culture have repressed their feelings to avoid the pain of rejection and inferiority wrapped around their father wounds. Consequently, they resist bringing them to the surface. Many have lost the capacity to identify their emotions after suppressing them for a long time, and that makes there exposure even more fearful. Whereas most women naturally draw closer to their feelings and explore them, most men are not so brave in dealing with feelings — and respond in the opposite way.

Men Evaluate and Women Emote

A Disclaimer: the men and women described in the previous and following sections may or may not be like you. Not all men or women are similar to this 'typical' model, decide for yourself, however, if the "shoe fits," we want you to know what to do.

One of the major differences in the way many men and women go through life is that women often relate by how they *feel* about things, while men more often relate by what they *think* of things. Women are also capable of processing things logically; the point is that many men process life primarily through the logical part of their brains rather than the emotional. Another difference between the sexes is made evident by the fact that, generally, women talk more than men. This is because women commonly, think verbally, so talking things through helps them to understand. Men, on the other hand, often prefer to process their thoughts in silence.

When men and women come to recognize the differences in the ways they interpret their world, they can move past unrealistic expectations of one another that can lead to gender bias. They can truly be helpmates and actually assist each other in working through the events of life. For example: in times of tragedy, like when a loved one is lost, a woman may express her grief passionately, whereas the man may remain silent and seek a place to be alone to work things through.

Men need to abandon the lie that crying or expressing feelings is womanly and unacceptable. God created men to experience and take pleasure in all the same emotions He experiences. We know from Scripture that "Jesus wept," felt sorrow, and compassion. God expressed numerous emotions throughout the Bible from love to hate, happiness to sadness, pleasure and pain, and more. If that makes God seem too "human," remember, we were made in *His* image, not He in ours.

Those who refuse to feel pain will not be able to experience the fullness of joy; those who refuse to allow feelings of rejection will not be able to experience feelings of love and acceptance. A man who buries every emotion deep inside and refuses to profit from them will not only suffer a great personal loss, but his family will be unable to connect with him through his barricade of detachment, denial, and emotional silence.

A Boy and His Dad

Other than godly instruction, boys primarily need two things from their fathers or father surrogates, but they need a lot of both of them:

1) *Affirmation and validation* — Boys need to be told many times, in hundreds of different ways, on every possible occasion (sometimes even using words):
   a) "I genuinely love you."
   b) "I'm proud of you and proud to be your father."
   c) "You've got what it takes to be a man."
   d) "Our family would not be complete without you."
   e) "God has a wonderful plan for your life."
   f) "My name and future are wrapped up in you."
   g) "You can accomplish important things."

2) *Communication about and demonstrations of manhood during shared activities* — Fathers need to find an activity to share exclusively with their sons. In former times, that kind of connection often occurred while working the family farm, or while hunting and fishing together. More recently, some fathers have bonded with their sons while working on automobiles. These traditional 'guy activities' may still work for some, but many men will need to find other interests to pursue with their sons.

It matters little what you and your son do together. It could be something as simple as working out in the gym as I (Bart) do with my eldest son. However, competitive sports that pit a boy against his father are generally not a good option. The purpose is to find common ground for communication and to create situations where bonding and trust can flourish.

During your time together, look for opportunities to accomplish two things:

1. Model — what it means to be a man, how men respond to issues, which issues are important, the core values of manhood, and other masculine things.

2. Affirm his value — show your affection, demonstrate your devotion to helping him deal with life's issues, and confirm that the two of you share a masculine relationship that is unique and different from his relationship with his mother or sister(s).

Fathers need to demonstrate to their sons, by leading in spiritual things, that being spiritual is what real men do. A son needs to see his dad pray, and learn from his him how to study God's Word. Also, a son should learn from his dad how to treat women, like his sister and mother and never be allowed to show disrespect to any woman.

Women Only

A mother may have to fight feelings of rejection when her son bonds more deeply with his father or a father-figure. However, she should try to remember that if she were included in these activities, the boy would not be able to make the deep connection that is vital for him to make with the soul and spirit of the father-figure in his life. Bonding at a deep level is vital because it provides the opportunity to …

- Brings to life the 'silent hero' in the boy
- Awakens his warrior nature
- Demonstrates how to rescue a woman in need
- Explains the things that make a man unique from a woman
- Describes when a man should hold on … when he should step aside … and when it is all right to run away

Mom, allowing your son to spend time with a father-figure is the best investment you can make into his future happiness and success.

A Boy and His Mom

Another disclaimer: the following section does not apply to every mother or to every son; however, the dynamics mentioned in this section are common in our culture. Again, only you can determine if they apply to you and to your situation.

A boy who becomes frustrated in his search for approval from his father may turn to his mother or another female to meet his needs and end up *over-bonding* with her or another female. A mother who watches her young son try unsuccessfully to connect with his father will naturally feel sympathetic and may try to make up for it by creating a *special relationship* with her son.

In much the same way that mommy desires to "make it better" when a knee gets scraped, a mother may try to mend emotional wounds caused by the father. However, she can trigger deep angry in her son by doing so. The only one who can make a man out of the boy is his father or some other father figure.

Although over-bonding of a mother with her son can be come from the good intentions, I believe it is a great problem in our culture because so many mothers are single and must raise their children alone. Over-bonding with a female soul can cause a boy to forget his need for a father's approval, stop his search for manhood, and result in slavery to a female soul. A young boy dominated by a female spirit will often become a weak man who lacks courage. A mother's love was never intended to satisfy a young male soul, and the long-term consequences of that condition can be devastating. I believe that a man who grows up over-bonding with his mother may ...

- Marry a woman who has strength and character instead of finding those qualities within himself
- Come to fear and even hate women, based on the belief that they are stronger than he is and want to dominate, manipulate, and control him.
- Find it difficult, as an adult, to have a healthy relationship with any woman
- Become trapped in dependent relationships with genuinely domineering women, crawling back to them again and again to get the acceptance he experienced from his mother.
- Because of hidden anger toward women, he may look for someone to domineer and violate.
- Have multiple sexual encounters as he searches for a woman who will give the feeling of approval he once had from his mom
- Have to deal with gender confusion, and possibly with homosexuality

Even in a normal mother-son relationship, there may come a time when she may challenge his masculinity by over emphasizing *security* over *risk*. Should this happen, it is crucial for the father to rescue the boy from his mother's well-meaning, but mistaken protectiveness. This 'rescue' is not only instructional but also validates that the boy's true identity lies with men and not women. Men need to teach boys that being courageous requires taking *necessary* risks.

A mother can actually thwart her son's progress toward manhood by being more concerned about his hurt 'feelings' than the 'lessons' he needs to learn. She may think the father is being too hard on the boy. (Please understand, abusive discipline is never appropriate.)

Women Only

I (Henry) remember a day when Bart and his family were visiting and my oldest grandson, who was about 4 years–old, wanted to climb a tree in the yard. His father said, "Yes, go for it!" but his mother insisted that he was too young and might fall and hurt himself. I put the boy on the first limb of the tree and encouraged him to climb higher while standing below to catch him should he fall. This example is only one instance why a father needs to take an active part in childrearing.

Spiritual Aspect of the Father Wound

You may recall I said earlier that I believe every man has a father wound. Even when a father meets his responsibilities of bring his son into manhood a boy still needs more than a father has to give. A young man can never get all that he needs from his *natural* father because there is a spiritual aspect to fatherhood that can be met only by his *Heavenly* Father.

God created man with a spirit so they could enjoy a continuous connection with one another. Through that intimate connection with the Heavenly Father, Adam (and Eve, for that matter) received all the acceptance and affirmation and validation they needed. The loss of this spiritual connection with God, due to their fall into sin, created the *spiritual* aspect of every person's *father wound*.

In the beginning, man was created as a three-part being. He had a body that connected him with the physical realm, a spirit that connected him to God, and soul which consisted of his mind, will, and emotions that allowed him to process input from the physical and spiritual realms. Originally, the spirit and soul were combined into a singular unit ruled by the spirit. Adam's sin, however, created a division between the spirit and soul, and this division is the spiritual source of the *father wound*. This injury can only be completely healed by returning to our *Heavenly* Father and receiving *His* affirmation and validation. Because men and women were created in God's likeness, only the Creator can heal the human spirit and soul, and truly connect men and women to Him, and to one another.

However, for this to happen, a connection with the Father must be restored. This is one of the reasons for the Cross: *"... God was in Christ reconciling the world to Himself..."* (II Corinthians 5:19 NKJV). Salvation through the blood of Jesus made reconciliation with God possible and positions us for healing and release from the father wound. However, this healing does not occur automatically at the moment of spiritual rebirth but must be pursued as part of an ongoing intimate relationship with God.

Women Only

Mom, one of the greatest gifts you can give to your son is to help facilitate his time together with his father or father figure. To the extent it is possible, help the father understand his son's need for his Dad's time and attention. Promote their time together.

Dilemma of the Wound Heart

The *father wound* has other significant spiritual ramifications. It can cause us to look for acceptance "in all the wrong places" and thereby commit sin. Sin is like an infection that must be purged from a wound before healing can occur.

When asked to name the most important of God's commandments, Jesus answered without hesitation: *"... You shall **love** the Lord your God **with all your heart**, and with **all your soul**, and with **all your mind**"* (Matthew 22:37 NASB, emphasis added). Anything we love more than God is idolatrous and therefore sin.

Let me (Henry) give you an example: I ministered to a young man, a senior in college, who tried to use football as the means of getting his dad's approval. Although his father had been a football star, his son was merely an average player. Sport became an idol to the son. He believed that the way to gain his father's approval was to become good at sports. The young man felt that his father's love and acceptance was performance based. By withholding his approval, the father tried to manipulate his son to perform better which pushed his son into idolatry and performance-based living.

We err when we try to cure our *father wound* by seeking approval from our father (and others) rather than from God. Jesus declared that He came to heal the brokenhearted, which includes father wounds:

> *The Spirit of the Lord is upon me, because he hath anointed me to preach the gospel to the poor;* **he hath sent me to heal the brokenhearted,** *to preach deliverance to the captives, and recovering of sight to the blind,* **to set at liberty them that are bruised,** (Luke 4:18 KJVA emphasis added).

Longing for approval can lead to sins which become habitual. Many men find things to provide short-term satisfaction of their needs for acceptance or that deaden the pain of rejection and insecurity. Self-medication can take the form of the misuse of drugs, sex, porn, alcohol, and other things. Whatever substitute we use is sinful, and we must repent and turn away from it.

The Perfect Papa

However, there is good news! In fact, it is *very* good news. The *father wound* can become the best example of how God *"makes all things work together"* for our good and for His glory, as says in Romans 8:28.

Even before Jesus purchased our freedom from woundedness, God proclaimed through David that He is a *"... Father to the fatherless ..."* (Psalms 68:5). A *father wound* makes you feel as if your father was 'less' than you needed. God will fill up those empty places where your dad was 'less' with His 'more than enough.' The Apostle Paul further explains:

> *For as many as are led by the Spirit of God, these are* **sons of God.** *For you did not receive a spirit of slavery again to fear, but* **you received a Spirit of adoption** *by which we cry, Abba! Father! The Spirit Himself witnesses with our spirit that* **we are children of God.** (Romans 8:14-16 LITV, emphasis added).

Like Adam, every person (male or female) was fashioned for sonship with God. Consequently, the needs of your heart can be completely satisfied only by bonding with your Father God and by receiving *His* affirmation and *His* validation. The "spirit of adoption" creates the basis for bonding with God and satisfying the spiritual aspects of the *father wound*.

First, you must seek forgiveness for your sins, especially those related to your *father wound*. Pray about ...

- The sin of seeking approval from others
- Forgiving your natural father and others who disappointed you
- The sinful behaviors you engaged in to satisfy your need for acceptance and to numb the pain of rejection.

Then, you must allow God to search your heart and reveal to you the actions, reactions, and attitudes that may seem natural (because you lived that way for so long) but are actually the result of your *father wound*. And, ask God to make you aware of when you act in those ways, or are about to, so that you can create new ways of acting and being.

You cannot fully become a man or live a life of true integrity manifesting Christian values until the 'root of your manhood' is purified by, and anchored in your Father God. As the Creator, He is the originator of masculinity and only He can properly root the male soul on a firm foundation which is free from guilt, shame, rejection, and insecurity. (God is also the creator of femininity and the only One Who can set the female soul free to be everything it was meant to be.)

I (Henry) once ministered to a fifty year-old man who was deeply broken because he had been a poor father. He was filled with shame, guilt, and feeling of failure. He had left the raising of his children to his wife and spent very little time with his son. Consequently, the son was severely father-wounded and felt that his Dad did not love or approve of him and his life-choices. There was a deep gulf between them. The father repented and went to his son and asked for forgiveness. Reconciliation was difficult for both of them, but they began a journey that eventual led to healing and a good relationship.

I (Henry) never received approval or affirmation from my earthly father; he was never a part of my life. He never hugged me, told me that he loved me, gave me a gift, contributed money toward my raising, or in any way acknowledged me as his son. I pastored for many years before I could let go of all that hurt and pain. Once healed of my deep father wound, however, I was able to draw closer to Father God and experience feelings of His love and acceptance in my soul.

Women Only

Although a woman will always be her son's mother, a time should come when mothering days are over and the son begins to relate to his mother in a different way. This can be a difficult transition for some mothers; it can make them feel as if they are losing their son, and cause them to hold on even harder. However, to continue to hold on when it is time to let go, may push a son eventually to rebel against his mother. This can result in a mother's missing out on the joys of having a close adult relationship with her son and his wife, and enjoying her grandchildren.

ACTION STEPS

1. Prayer Point:
God, I recognize my need for healing and give You permission to act in my life. I am open for You to set me on the road to freedom and healing. I choose to forgive and release my father and others who have disappointed and hurt me. Father, I trust You because I know that you are good and have the best of intentions toward me. I ask you to heal my broken heart, recreate my manhood, and fuse my human spirit with the spirit of adoption that comes from you. Amen.

2. Get in a quiet place and write a letter to your father, whether he is living or dead. Explain how you feel about him as a father and give details about your woundedness. (This exercise will allow you to understand the issues of your father wound and to experience buried pain. You must *know* your issues to be released from them.)

Normally, you would not mail this letter but rather consider it an exercise. Next, you should pray and ask Father God to give you a right perspective and bring to your memory every issue from your relationship with your father that needs forgiveness. (Also, ask Him to remind you of the ways your father showed genuine affection for you.)

3.   You may need to find a 'safe place' and you may need 'help' to work through difficult issues. There are several ministries that can be helpful to you:

- Elijah House Ministries
- Vision Life Ministry
- Prayer Ministry Network and other ministries that emphasis the healing of the spirit and soul

These ministries hold seminars and have ministry products that you would find useful: The following books may also be helpful:

Healing the Masculine Soul by Gordon Dalbey

Shadow Boxing by Henry Malone

God's Power to Change: Healing the Wounded Spirit by John Sanford

4.   If your son is still at home, begin immediately to apply the principles of this chapter: affirm and create "common ground" with him. Make a regular appointment with him to do something you both enjoy. Give him all the time he needs to bond with you. (There is no substitute for your time, as a father, and no more important way to spend it.) Look for opportunities to demonstrate how a godly man deals with the issues of life. Remember that your son is always watching how you model manhood. If your son is grown and lives away from home, it is not too late to give him your approval, affirmation, and validation.

5.   As you consider the way you have raised your son, you may discover that you should go to him and ask his forgiveness for the times that your actions failed to measure up to his needs.

▪▪▪

In the next chapter ...

We talk about a subject of interest to almost everyone, S-E-X. We will seek answers to the question: If sex was created by God and intended to be a good thing for men and women, then why can it be such a problem for a man trying to live the Christian life, and what can you do about it?

Chapter 3
What's Love Got To Do With 'It'?

Sexuality is a gift from God intended to bless. Yet for many conscientious Christian men and women (both married and single), it can seem more like a curse. Where are we missing it? How can we redeem our sexuality so it can be the blessing God intended?

Some of the struggles that Christian men and women face with their sexuality have been highlighted in recent polls:

- Dr. Archibald Hart talked to more than 600 Christian men on the topic of masturbation and discovered:
    - 61% of married Christian men masturbate
    - 82% of those men have 'self-sex' an average of once a week
    - 13% said they felt it was normal.

- In a recent poll by *Today's Christian Woman*, an online newsletter, 34 percent of female readers, admitted to intentionally accessing Internet porn.

- The website of Rick Warren, author of the *Purpose Driven Life*, surveyed porn usage by pastors. Of the 1351 men who responded:
    - 54% had viewed Internet porn in the last year
    - 30% had visited porn websites within the last 30 days.

WOMEN ONLY

A Ladies Home Journal survey found that 47% of women who responded reported using erotica or pornography to heighten their sexual experience. Perhaps you have heard Woody Allen's famous one-liner: "Sex without love is an empty experience, but as empty experiences go, it's one of the best." Many who use pornography would say the same thing. Why are people driven to pursue something more in their sexuality?

Could the drive that causes women (and men) to seek out pornography actually come from a deep-seated feeling that something essential is missing from their sexual experience? Could they actually be looking in the wrong place for satisfaction that only God's plan for sexuality can provide?

Followers of Christ have a message for pornography users: there is something far better than porn, it's the real deal — sex within the marriage covenant that goes beyond mere lust fulfillment. The real thing brings love and intimacy to all three levels of the human nature: spirit, soul, and body.

Sexuality In the Image of God

The Bible says:

> God created man in His own image, in the image of God He created him; male and female He created them. God blessed them; and God said to them, "Be fruitful and multiply, and fill the earth ... (Genesis 1:27,28 NASB).

From this scripture, it is obvious that God blessed man and woman (before they sinned) with the ability to have sex and children. Consequently, sexuality must be considered a blessing. In addition, at the close of this creation day, God announced that what He had made was "good." To rediscover the blessing of sex, we have to learn to differentiate good sexuality from bad so that we can cultivate the good.

Have you ever wondered where sexuality came from? The seeds of sexuality had to be somewhere within the Trinity to have found its place in mankind.

But, how could we receive sexuality from a God who is not sexual in the human sense? Some of the aspects of God, when combined synergistically in humanity express themselves in sexuality; qualities like ...

- The desire to love and be love
- The desire for intimacy
- The desire to create

WOMEN ONLY

God gave to women the purest expression of the three aspects of human sexuality to propagate the human species. Love between a man and woman creates the desire for intimacy; intimacy is sometimes expressed through sexual intercourse; and from intercourse, a child may be created.

Our spirit, soul, and body express the aspects of God-given sexuality differently:

The human spirit — longs for **love and intimacy** with God and desires to collaborate with Him in a **creative** way. God made each of us for a purpose which is beyond our ability and attainable only when we **co-create** with God.

The human soul — desires **loving** relationships with various levels of **intimacy** depending on the type of relationship. We each have a need to be united with people of like mind and with a life-partner of the opposite gender. Men and women express their sexuality in different ways: man is often the aggressor and pursues, while a woman's nature is to respond. However, a wife can also initiate intimacy.

The human body — views everything through a filter of pleasure and pain. It is drawn to that which gives it pleasure and repelled by those things that give it pain. At this unsophisticated level of perception, the desire for **love**, **intimacy**, and **creativity** is lumped together and crudely defined as S-E-X! Most people only know sexuality from this definition. Many are seduced by their craving for pleasure to pursue Satan's counterfeits to love, intimacy, and creativity, lust and fantasies.

To experience sexuality as the blessing God intended, we must first reconnect with the Spirit of God by becoming born-again, then realign ourselves with God's original plan for sexual intimacy and allow it to redefine our sexuality. This realignment is not automatic but comes through a partnership with God's power and a Christian's will to reestablish the authority of the human spirit over the body and soul.

WOMEN ONLY

Sex & Shame: Both women and men often have negative issues connected with their sexuality. Shame in many cases is linked to a negative experience. If the cause was incest, seduction, or rape, the shame can be so great it creates an emotional mountain that a normal relationship may find impossible to scale.

Until inner healing is received by a person suffering from shame, their attitude toward the opposite sex and sexuality can be warped. Researchers say that as many as 80% of women and 60% of men have had strongly negative sexual experiences by age 19. Hence, it is no surprise that many Christian people have difficulty in this area.

Sex in Marriage: Some women marry with dreams of a loving husband who will change their lives and give them the security and acceptance they crave; but they may find that their husband cannot deliver on their dreams. To make matters worse, some wives discover that the emotions which initially encouraged their desire for sex — a craving for closeness and intimacy — lessen when those things elude them. An unsuccessful attempt to create intimacy may decrease a woman's desire for sex while her husband's sexual desires may increase if he is sexually deprived. This can create a downward spiral in their relationship that could lead to divorce.

Should they not find sexual satisfaction in marriage, women, (and men) may try extramarital affairs and/or pornography. However, neither will fulfill a person's desires over the long run. The real solution is to building a fulfilling, intimate sexual relationship with their spouse.

People should not expect a 'quick fix' because developing a healthy sexuality can require healing in dysfunctional areas, discipline, and a commitment to the overall process. The key to sexual satisfaction for many women is finding healing in areas of defilement and shame. Without healing, they will never be able to find the intimacy they desire

Satan's Unsatisfactory Sham — Sensuality

God is a Creator, but satan is not, he can only copy, corrupt, or counterfeit. Satan's imitation of sexuality is *sensuality,* and his counterfeit of love is *lust.* Sensuality is often a zesty concoction of mystery, intrigue, suggestiveness, the provocative, and the erotic all spiced with secrecy. Consequently, the definitions of love and romance in our society have been corrupted by the elements of lust and sensuality.

Because our culture, for the most part, has accepted this flawed definition, many Christian men and women looking for the *real* thing will first have to rediscover the true meaning of sexuality. Otherwise a monogamous marriage relationship with appropriate sexuality can seem unexciting to Christians brainwashed by the world's standards. As a result, Christian men and women can be seduced into going outside of marriage to satisfy a desire for sexual 'thrills.'

The forbidden always has great appeal; the grass on the other side of the fence is inevitably greener. Yet, once a person steps over the boundaries of monogamy, all they find is someone also searching for intimacy but with no understanding of how to attain it. Yes, lust and extra-marital relationships may give pleasure for the moment, but the relationship inevitably becomes unfulfilling and the person goes on to the next one. They continue looking for *real* intimacy without recognizing what is missing, never making progress only 'jogging in-place' within the limits of their ignorance.

The Bible calls the thoughts of sexual thrill-seekers "vain imaginations," and "futile speculations" and warns in Roman 1:21-32, that this kind of thinking leads to a "depraved mind." The addiction to erotic fantasy is one of the things at the root of a fascination with pornography.

Those who believe they need the erotic in their sex life can never find a *natural* relationship with their spouse to be satisfactory. In the real world, women will not do the degrading things graphically depicted as typical in pornography. If a person's marriage is not fulfilling their needs, before they blame their spouse, they should ask themselves if what they consider a 'sexual need' is pornographic and demeaning to the person they love. Scripture states that there is no end to the desires of lust, and that it becomes a bottomless pit which eventually swallows those who fall into it. Sensuality allows the body and soul to rule the sex life. Yet, those who find the *real* thing discover that sex is *spiritual,* as well as, physical and emotional.

I (Henry) once ministered to a woman who searched outside her marriage for true love. Her husband was hooked on porn and used her only for his satisfaction. He often required her do things that she felt were perverted and degrading. She began to look for someone who would love and value her as a person, not just a 'thing.' She worked with a man who had reached out to her and helped her get vocation retraining.

Their relationship began pure but she was soon comparing his kindness with her husband's lack of respect. All the things that were missing in her husband, she found in this man. They began spending more and more time together at work. They had lunch together as often as possible. One day she invited him to skip lunch and take her to a hotel. He accepted and that was the beginning of their affair. She came to me after realizing that her affair failed to give her any more satisfaction than her relationship with her husband. Initially, she came for healing of her father wound. Once that was healed, she was able to work with her husband to create a mutually satisfying marriage.

WOMEN ONLY
Our culture conveys to women that they are unacceptable as they are naturally, and must be sexy. However, in the end, no woman can ever possibly measure up to this impossible ideal for allure and attractiveness (except a few scrawny models that have probably undergone multiple cosmetic surgeries).

The feeling of inadequacy that results from a woman comparing herself to an unrealistic ideal can result in eating disorders, addictions, and other obsessive behaviors. God never intended a woman to be like a porn star or pop diva. They are mere fabrications — more myth than reality! This goal of sexiness is unreachable for all but a few. Those woman who do reach it, find that it is unfulfilling and degrading.

Women who succeed in becoming part of a man's fantasies actually become unreal to him, merely a performer in his sexual imaginations. Men who live in their fantasies are like drug addicts who always require more, more of things that no woman really wants to give (and no man who loves his woman should ever ask). This is not God's way!

Female Hollywood stars that attain the status of a Sex Goddess are illustrations of the futility of this life. Many of them have surgery after surgery, and go from one man to the next, never finding what they are looking for because there is no lasting fulfillment in being able to gratify a man's 'vain imaginations.' Unfortunately, many times their personal lives become more tragic than any role they could play.

Some people feel there is something fundamentally shameful about sex, but it was never a disgraceful thing to God. Adam and Eve, before their fall, were naked and felt no shame, and God have a problem with it. He even encouraged them to have intercourse to propagate the race. Within the context of marriage, sex is not only appropriate but required to establish the intimacy necessary for "two to become one." Unless misunderstandings about sex are corrected, they will cause a husband and wife to miss out on the blessing of their marriage.

WOMEN ONLY
'Secret sex' can create a false idea that is damaging to an understanding of what makes for truly 'good sex.'

The excitement of sneaking around and doing what is forbidden, that some have experienced, is opposite to the openness that good sex requires.

Those who want the thrill of 'living on the edge' should take up skydiving because real sexual fulfillment requires an intimacy that only openness between a husband and wife, who love one another, makes possible. Allowing the thrill of 'secret sex' into the definition of good sex can lead to promiscuity with attractive strangers and ultimately to emptiness and disillusionment.

A Lusty Kind of Love

Few men or women receive an education in *love* while growing up, but many get lots of instructions in *lust*. Here are some fundamental truths about sexuality you may have missed:

- God designed sexual intimacy to be born out of love.
- Love can always wait to have its needs met, but lust can never wait.
- Sexuality that comes from anything but love is mere sensuality, satan's counterfeit.
- Being married does not mean that you have your sexuality straightened out.
- Sex with your spouse that is motivated by lust, rather than love, is still just lust and will never bring the deep satisfaction either of you desire.
- You can misinterpret your 'sexual urges' and think that a desire for *real intimacy* is a need for more sex.
- The desire for greater intimacy with God can be misunderstood as a desire for sex.

WOMEN ONLY

Hollywood, advertising, news media, sex magazines, and the women's movement have exploited the women. They have promoted the idea that an enlightened woman is sexually liberated and entitled to be just as lusty as a man, rather than a person of godly character (as men should also be). Many women have been brainwashed to believe that 'purity' is a prudish, old-fashioned idea and that has caused a twisted view of sex.

I (Henry) have ministered to a number of women who yielded to peer pressure to give away their virginity at an early age. Virginity, however, is a treasure meant to be given to a life-mate. Don't allow anything or anyone to cause you to treat it as a valueless anomaly.

Defiling the Marriage Bed

What you do in the marriage bed does *not* dishonor it, but rather what you do outside it. The writer of Hebrews put it like this:

> *Marriage is to be held in honor among all, and the marriage bed is to be undefiled; for fornicators and adulterers God will judge* (Hebrews 13:4 NASB).

The marriage bed is a symbol for intimacy between husband and wife. To make yourself *truly* naked before your spouse is to become transparent and vulnerable which requires trust. Infidelity, by either one, violates that trust and destroys the purity of this precious and unique relationship. Even when it is forgiven, infidelity can leave a scar requiring years to heal. Clearly, God expects us to guard and preserve the blessing of sexuality by remaining faithful to our spouses.

Different couples enjoy doing different things sexually, and most anything which is mutually enjoyable and not harmful is okay. The question is not so much *what* you do but *why* you do it:

- Are you making love to your spouse or just using them to give yourself pleasure?
- Do you need to look at porn to get excited enough for sex with your spouse?

- Do you insist on doing unnatural things that you've seen in pornography?
- Do you need to use sexual toys?
- Do you regularly engage in masturbation?
- Does your husband or wife fail to satisfy you sexually?

If any of the above is true, then as a Christian man or woman, you may have issues concerning your sexuality you need to deal with. Often the best answer is to get Christian counseling, and the place to begin, for most people, is your pastor.

WOMEN ONLY
Many women, who have problems with lust that I (Henry) have ministered to were abused during childhood, their sexuality was aroused long before God intended. They had to deal with such feelings without the mental and emotional maturity (and the spiritual understanding) to do so. Lust took hold of their life and yet, when they tried to use it to satisfy deeper needs for love, appreciation, and acceptance, they found only emptiness and shame. If that describes you, God wants to heal you.

Masturbation and Pornography
Many Christian men (and some women) consider masturbation okay or at least preferable to sexual frustration or having illicit sex. Although the physical act is not *directly* mentioned in the Bible, it is clear from scripture that God always considers sex other than with your spouse to be immoral. In addition, masturbation is a favorite method used to obtain physical gratification by those who indulge in pornography.

Porn creates shame, often subconsciously, in men because it portrays women in unnatural ways. When a person witnesses the degradation of a woman's body for the purpose of lust, his mental participation makes him guilty of the behavior witnessed. The degrading of one's sexuality can become an ongoing process going from bad to worse. Porn is like a drug that gives pleasure but never completely satisfies; it holds out the promise that more will finally bring fulfillment.

Some argue that pornography is a victimless offense. Setting aside the fact that women in the porn industry are often poorly used and abused, the most wounded are not the individual themselves but their marriage, their spouse, and their children. Few spouses can compete in physical attractiveness or equal the unnatural acts found in pornography. Consequently, the spouses of those who participate in it are made to feel inadequate.

Their spouse's often reason, "If I were able to truly satisfy my mate sexually, they wouldn't need pornography." That assessment, however, is mistaken because it does not take into account porn's addictive nature that can never leads to *lasting* satisfaction. No picture or movie can ever give what they desire. That kind of satisfaction requires another human being to open their spirit and soul to you. It is much more than momentary physical pleasure.

The *real* deal is experienced when two people become intimately connected in all three realms of their being — spirit, soul, and body. That scope of satisfaction is exactly what God intended when He gave sexuality to mankind.

WOMEN ONLY
Many women find pleasure and a measure of satisfaction in giving their men pleasure even though they may not reach climax themselves. A woman, however, should encourage her husband to work with her to create a good vaginal orgasm during lovemaking.

Sex and the Single Person
In a culture that considers it "normal" for single men and women to sleep together, the truth remains: sex outside of marriage is still sin. And like every other form of sin, it exacts a high price.

Living together and casual sex …
> *Devalues the sanctity of marriage* by using something for self-satisfaction that God intended to express love and create a bond within marriage.

Cheapens both men and women by causing them to become mere objects of each other's lust. It promotes a description of a person based solely on physical attributes and skill at performing sexually and it overlooks more meaningful characteristics. It makes personal relations one dimensional and shallow.

Hardens your heart toward the person used for pleasure. They become a _toy_ rather than a human being with needs and feelings. It destroys a man's or woman's self-worth because their shame devalues them.

Fractures your spirit and soul as your spirit co-mingles with sexual partners. Your soul becomes splintered with each 'soul tie' created with sex partners. These often become beachheads where the enemy can creates strongholds. Paul said in I Corinthians 6:16:

> _Or do you not know that he who is joined to a prostitute becomes one body with her? For, as it is written, "The two will become one flesh"_ (ESV).

Soul ties can make the marriage bed feel very crowded. Your spouse may sense this, consciously or unconsciously, and be made uncomfortable or insecure. Even if you have forgotten your former sexual partners, you remain connected with them until you make the effort to break the ties created with them.

I (Henry) once ministered to a man who never learned the value of sexual purity. Growing up, all he saw modeled was guys having as much sex with as many partners as possible. He adopted that as his lifestyle and had one sexual encounter after another, never remaining in any relationship for very long. During college, he fell in 'lust' with a beautiful girl and they married but were never able to really bond in soul and spirit. She, like all his other bed partners, was merely an outlet for his lust and sexual gratification.

Eventually, they had three children but, never having developed a deep connection with his wife, he was drawn to other women and began to again have affairs. After 15 years, their marriage ended in divorced. A major reason for their lack of intimate was the many 'soul ties' he had created. His soul was shattered and his marriage bed was haunted by connections forged with other women.

Severing Soul Ties

Soul ties can be broken and, in fact, they must be severed for a man or woman to enjoy *real* sexual intimacy with their spouse. To become free, pray the following prayer aloud, and with meaning for each person who formed a sexual connection with:

> *Father God, thank you for saving me from destruction. I confess that I have sinned and in Jesus' name, I renounce and sever ungodly soul ties formed between myself and (name). Please heal my soul of any wounds and reintegrate the part of me that was deposited in the other person and restore me to wholeness. I ask that you also restore the person with whom I sinned to wholeness. I rebuke any evil spirits that have found a foothold in me because of this soul tie, and I command them to leave me and never to return. Thank you, Lord for your healing, restoring power, and for your perfect love for me, Amen.*

If you would like more information about soul ties, or need further help breaking them, contact a prayer ministry like Elijah House. You can also find more information on soul ties in the following book, *Seductions Exposed — The spiritual dynamic of relationships* by Dr. Gary Greenwald.

WOMEN ONLY

Women need an exclusive place of security with their men, a place they share intimacy that no other person is able to reach. Soul ties with previous lovers create a breach in that place and can keep a woman (or man) from the intimacy they need and desire.

Women are more likely than men to forgive adultery. Adultery hurts men in a deeper way than women, which makes it more difficult for them to recover. Through my ministry I (Henry) have found that anyone, man or woman, can forgive a spouse who has committed adultery when they understand that forgiveness is a choice not a feeling. When they realize forgiveness is not optional but a requirement of God. And when they understand that forgiveness is not a naive reinstatement of trust (trust has to be earned). Those who will not deal with their hurt, anger, and unforgiveness and refuse to receive healing from God are described in the Bible as having 'hard hearts' and usually divorce their spouses.

Sexuality, Spirituality, and Fasting

In 1 Corinthians 7:5, Paul says a curious thing:

> *Stop depriving one another, except by agreement for a time, so that you may devote yourselves to prayer, and come together again so that Satan will not tempt you because of your lack of self-control* (NASB).

This scripture alludes to something hardly mentioned in the modern church: the fasting from sexual relations with your spouse. However, some Christian leaders, both past and present, say that their spiritual growth was stunted until their sexual passions were harnessed through a fast from sex. Such a fast, allows a person to more easily channel their passion for intimacy into their relationship with the Lord.

If you struggle with sexual thoughts, with mental pictures that flash into your mind and seem beyond control, there is an answer — fast all media for a time and replacing it with Bible reading and meditating on God's Word. The "washing of the water of the Word" will cleanse, purify, and give you back control over your mind.

WOMEN ONLY

We all need to bring our thoughts captive to Jesus. We cannot allow our minds to run wild and think any thought that floats into our consciousness. We have to guard our hearts from a constant diet of television programs, books, etc. where adultery is a common theme. How naïve we are to think that we can invite the devil's harmful substitute for God's sexuality into our minds, and not have it shape our thoughts and beliefs.

The "Other Woman" (or Man)

Statistics show that affairs occur most often between people who encounter one another on a regular basis. Because most man and women work with people of the opposite sex, we need a strategy for dealing with this source of temptation. By setting a few boundaries, and following simple guidelines, everyone can keep such relationships from threatening their marriage.

One key to eliminating the *other women* (or other men) in your life as a sexual temptation is to view them as if they were a family member. Categorize all colleagues of the opposite gender into one of three categories, and relate to them accordingly:

Father- or mother -like (an older man or woman or one in authority)

Brother- or sister-like (co-worker of the same age)

Son- or daughter-like (a younger person or subordinate)

This method makes it possible for men and women to have close working relationships with members of the opposite sex without it threatening their marriage.

Following are additional guidelines to help minimize risky behavior with *other* women or men:

- Never discuss anything personal with someone of the opposite sex that you have not already discussed with your spouse. To do so, creates a false emotional bond that rivals the marital bond of intimacy with your spouse.
- Never discuss *any* aspect of your marriage — or theirs.
- Do not spend extended periods of time *alone* with a person of the opposite gender. Arrange to have others present, hold your meetings in public places, or plan several short meetings to replace a length one. If you feel *any* attraction to the man or woman with whom you are meeting then you *must never* make exception to this guideline.
- If you find yourself looking at the body of a man or woman you work with or having sexual thoughts or fantasies about them, you need to step back and say to your lusts a determined, "NO!" You are in a wrong place in your mind and you must deal with it immediately. Lust is easier to manage when plucked out early, like a weed before it matures and reproduces itself.
- Put down imaginations of the 'ideal' husband, wife, or sex partner. Refuse to evaluate every man or woman you meet, including your husband or wife, against this fantasy. Unconsciously, every man creates a vision of the ideal woman and every woman does the same. Remind yourself that your fantasy-woman or fantasy-man is merely an unrealistic *dream* person who does not exist and never could. So laugh off your cartoon caricature of the ultimate mate and *get real*.

(I (Bart) have had many assistants over the years, both in business and ministry, and worked closely with many women who were not my wife. I have discovered that it is tempting to allow a person of the opposite sex to make you feel good about yourself, or fill a need that your spouse, or the Lord is not currently filling.

Once, I had an assistant who started telling others in the office that she really enjoyed working with me. She, also, mentioned how much she respected me. This progressed to the point of her asking my advice about issues regarding her relationship with her husband, and sharing intimate details about their marriage.

I was conflicted because the woman was very good at her position, a hard worker who needed the job for her family income. In addition, I had invested a lot of time training her and did not want to spend that time training another person. However, I recognized that no matter what I wanted, things were heading in the wrong direction and I had to address the issue. First, I discussed it with my wife, Kim, and we decided that if the woman crossed the line again in any way — verbally, emotionally, or physically — I would have to let her go.

A few days later, the woman pulled me aside to tell me she had fallen in love with me. Even though it would have been easy to put off firing her until I could find a replacement, I let her go that afternoon. Solomon, once wrote that only a fool holds fire to his chest and does not expect his clothes to be burned (see Proverbs 6:27).

Obviously, satan wants you to satisfy your *legitimate* sexual needs in *illegitimate* ways. Then he wants to use sin to separate you from God, and drown you in guilt and shame to prevent you from fulfilling your destiny. He will also try to harden your heart against your spouse because divorce results from a hard heart. To avoid becoming hardhearted make Ephesians 4:26 a rule in your marriage: *"... Do not let the sun go down on your anger"* (NASB).

WOMEN ONLY

Some women find it difficult to be honest with their husbands about sexual dissatisfaction, a reluctance that may come from insecurity about their relationship or fear of rejection. However, if a woman will learn how to express feeling of dissatisfaction to her spouse without making him feel belittled, she will overcome a significant hurdle in marital communication and improve her sexual satisfaction.

Women should be careful not to look to other men for security or emotional support, even if they are not getting it from their husbands. To do so can create an improper emotional bond and many women are tempted to have affairs because of that attachment. This is why some women have sexual affairs with the husbands of their best friends. He is a man they have became familiar and comfortable with. One day, the affair 'just seems to happen' without conscious planning or forethought.

Five Secrets to Super Sex For Men

When you discover God's original intentions for your sexuality, you will uncover a level of intimacy you never thought possible. Following are some helpful hints that can lead to the sex life you always wanted:

1. Create an atmosphere where love can flourish. Honor your wife's needs by doing things that she will find conducive to intimacy. Some women like candles, baths, etc. but the real secret is finding things that are *mutually* exciting.
2. Let your spouse know ahead of time if you have expectations of a romantic evening. Thus, you allow her to make the necessary mental adjustment, organize her schedule, and deal with children, and other things so that she can be comfortable with a time of sexual intimacy. The surprise thing — "Baby, I've been thinking about you all day. Let's do IT!" — does not work well for most women. Remember, your most important sex organ is your brain — use it *first*.
3. If she is not climaxing during intercourse, you must find out what is wrong and work on the problem (even if she claims it's okay). A candid discussion about things she enjoys in bed and doesn't will often help. *Putting her physical needs ahead of yours will guarantee*

getting you're needs met. Remember, as a Christian man you have been promised the Fruit of the Spirit called "self-control." No, I'm not kidding ... use it!

4. Keep in mind that *real satisfaction* is not about the mechanics of sex (positions and techniques, potions and lotions) but about the emotional engagement, the affection, and intimacy expressed during intercourse. The feminine nature is intuitive and will know if your sexuality is coming from a heart full of love or a mind high on lust. If she perceives that you are truly offering love and intimacy, she will open herself freely and give to you in return.

5. When sexual intimacy finds expression in all three areas — spirit, soul, and body — you can get so much sexual fulfillment during one session of love-making, that you will be satisfied for longer than you thought possible. You will even find yourself reminiscing about it with pleasure for days. *Real* love-making isn't obsessive but *really* fulfilling.

I (Bart) have a close friend in his late 40's who had never married but gone from one woman to another with little commitment beyond mutual sexual gratification. After he received Christ, he changed and abandoned his wanton ways. He and a longtime girl-friend, who had also recently become a Christian, decided to marry. He asked for my advice about how to keep sex fresh and exciting while remaining monogamous. Previously, his answer had been to continually change bed partners.

I shared with him that I had been married for 17 years, at that point, and never cheated on my wife, and we did not need sexual toys or aids to make our love life terrific. Because we had *real* love for one another, our love making was better than when we first married. He looked at me in astonishment and promptly asked me to do their pre-marriage counseling.

WOMEN ONLY
According to Patsy Rae Dawson, author of Marriage: A Taste of Heaven, Vol. II: God's People Make the Best Lovers; both secular and Christian surveys have shown that believers make the best lovers.

She says that a Christian couple can be truly uninhibited because they have the blessing of a clear conscience and, consequently, can enjoy their spouses to the fullest.

Christian women should embrace their sexuality with the realization that almost any sex act that is not harmful and is acceptable to both parties within the confines of marriage, is suitable and healthy. True sexual liberation for such women is the ability to not only welcome but also initiate intimate love with their husbands.

Five things a Christian woman can do to enjoy a more passionate love life:

1. Flirt with him — Jerry B. Jenkins, a marriage and family author, suggests working to cultivate the kinds of moments you had when first married. He calls it, "Things that made you rush home to tear off your clothes."

2. Remember your most satisfying times together — revisit the memories of great sex with your husband every time you make love. (A University of Chicago study found that Protestant women are the most likely to report achieving orgasm during intercourse.)

3. Be playful in bed — tease, tickle, touch and make a game of lovemaking. A woman who commits to making sex more exciting for her partner also makes it better for herself, and shows her man how important she consider his happiness to be.

4. Surprise him — make variety a part of your sex life by not only trying new things but looking for opportunities to make love at unusual times and in various situations. Don't let the bed become the only place, or night the only time, that you make love.

5. Be willing to adjust during lovemaking — there are moments to be gentle and loving, but there are times to be wildly passionate — go with the flow.

The most important tip for great sex is love. The above suggestions will enhance a sexual relationship but, without love, sex will never be ultimately fulfilling. Make each intimate time together more than mere sex ... a celebration of your love for one another.

Action Steps

1. Work on deepening your intimacy with your wife by talking to her about something important to you that you have been reluctant to mention before. It should be a something deeply meaningful that makes you feel vulnerable. If you have issues about your sexual relations then you should bring that up to her. However, any conversation about sex should *not* be intended to manipulate her into bed. The goal is not to 'get laid' or to even to 'win' an argument, but to give to her a part of yourself in intimacy, without expecting anything in return.

2. Following your talk, journal a paragraph (or more) about what happened during the discussion. This will help you look objectively at your feelings and at her reaction to your attempt to deepen the intimacy between you. Following that answer these question:
   - Why was my talk successful or unsuccessful?
   - What could I have done differently to make it better?
   - What did I learn about my wife's feelings, desires, and needs during this conversation?

3. Based on what you have learned about how to have a proper relationship with *other* women, list things that you need to do differently.

4. What can you do to create a *better* atmosphere for love to flourish in your home? Make a list of at least 10 ways you can show your spouses that your desire for intimacy comes from a heart of love. (Hint: think of ways to heighten the romance in your relationship.)

5. Pray over your wife. This may seem odd but it isn't; a woman wants to have a deeply spiritual connection to the man with whom she makes love. Pray for her aloud in her presence so she can hear what you are saying to God about her. She wants to know that she has a deep abiding place in your heart and that you care enough to pray for her.

OH, and if you haven't dealt with those soul ties to past relationships yet, go back to that page and take care of it now! They are real, and it is really important.

In the next chapter ...
We talk about temptations that are common to men (and women). You will discover that the New Covenant redefined sin — the bar has been raised. We will talk more about sex, from the temptation standpoint, but also discuss other temptations that can be just as challenging for men and women.

Chapter 4
Temptations Common to Men & Women

Let's talk about the temptations that men and women face — and ways to overcome them. How we deal with temptation is a very sensitive issue with God. Jesus considered this area so important He included it in the Lord's Prayer when He said, " *...do not let us yield to temptation...* " (see Matthew 6:9-13 NLT).

It was Adam and Eve's failure to deal correctly with temptation which cost them everything they valued — their intimacy with God and their home in the Garden of Eden — and caused their descendents to receive the birthmark of sin. However, Jesus' victory over temptation made it possible for Him to fulfill His divine purpose to become the Savior of humanity. *How we handle our temptations will decide whether we succeed (or fail) to fulfill our purpose*. (Each person should make a solemn vow to God, and to himself or herself, that they will do whatever it takes to finish well.) Should we fail to finish well, it will not matter how we began. On the other hand, if we finish strong, a poor start becomes irrelevant.

Everyone knows of Dr. Billy Graham's success and how he has finished well. At the beginning of his ministry, however, Billy was not expected to be the most successful of four young preachers who began at the same time. In fact, he was considered the least talented of the four. But, because he followed the ways of God, applied spiritual principles to his life, and made himself accountable, he finished ahead of his peers. One of the men gave up his destiny within 5 years of entering ministry and tried to become a movie star, but failed. Another man's ministry was ruined by lust and alcohol. The third man sold out to money. Dr. Graham, however, remained true to his calling. His name eventually became a household word, he became the spiritual advisor to several Presidents, and shared the gospel face-to-face with more people than any man in history.

Whether you believe satan is a mighty spiritual being or a paper tiger, you will probably agree that he has two powerful things working for him when he tempts us:

> First, he is more cunning, devious, and crafty than we are.
> Second, he knows all our 'hot buttons' (our areas of weakness).

Since the devil appears to have some advantage over us, you might wonder how we can expect to successfully overcome his temptations and those that come from our flesh. You *can* successfully overcome temptation! First, let's consider our initial reaction to them.

How Do You React to Temptation?
There are only three possible ways to respond — concede, ignore, and fight:

1. *Concede*: Take the course of least resistance and give in to your temptations. This is the route most men and women take and they justify it by thinking "everyone does it."

   I (Henry) recall a conversation with a business man who made a revealing statement. He knew I was a pastor and, as we discussed various things, we eventually got to the topic of honesty in business. He told me he was an upstanding, church-going fellow with high character and integrity. Then promptly shared that he rarely lied — to his customers, employees, or his wife — only when he really needed to! What an indictment of our society when the standard of high character is "not lying except when you have to."

2. *Ignore:* This response to temptation takes us to a dangerous place called 'denial.' Continuously giving into a temptation desensitizes us to the convicting voice of the Holy Spirit and to our human conscience.

Sinning becomes an automatic response to certain temptations. We push the knowledge of our wrongdoing below the consciousness level to get relief from feelings of guilt and shame, and those areas of life become blind spots — places we can no longer discern the truth. As you continue to read this chapter, ask the Lord to reveal any sins you have hidden from yourself.

As an example: I (Henry) ministered to a woman and her husband who had lost their zeal and become slack in their walk with God. The husband was a pastor and his wife a leader in their church. They looked for ways to relax at home after a hard day of ministry and began to have a second and third glass of wine each night. Also under the excuse of "unwinding," they began watching movies that they had previously refused avoided because of the sexual content. Before long, they were watching soft porn to help their sex life. The defiling of their conscience had shutoff the flow of the Spirit and the Lord's presence. Soon, they were unable to stop — even though they knew what they were doing was wrong. I led them to repent for their sins and, after a time, they were restored to a new and fresh relationship with God.

3. *Fight:* Christ expects His followers to go beyond 'conceding' and 'ignoring' temptation to fight and overcome the enticement to sin. The good news is that He has promised to limit our temptations to what we can withstand and help us through them:
   - *No temptation has overtaken you but such as is common to man; and ...*
   - *God is faithful, who will not allow you to be tempted beyond what you are able, ...*
   - *But with the temptation will provide the way of escape also, so that you will be able to endure it* (1 Corinthians 10:13 NASB).

In addition, God pledges to mount a rescue mission for those who stand firm during their trials and refuse to give in: *"... The Lord knows how to rescue the godly from temptation ..."* (II Peter 2:9 NASB).

WOMEN ONLY

Temptation is universal; women must deal with it, too. This is an area where a husband and wife can be a great benefit or hindrance to each other depending on their level of intimacy. Because many women (and men for that matter) consider their temptations as shameful, most are reluctant to discuss them openly with their spouses. Despite that, we come to know each other's strengths and weaknesses.

If you trust that your spouse would never knowingly hurt you, then you can ask him to help by holding you accountable. With this trust comes the responsibility not to use this sensitive information to manipulate or betray their trust by sharing it with anyone! If you or your spouse is not quite ready for that level of openness, then you can pray for one another to overcome weakness.

The Bible says: "... Confess your sins to one another, and pray for one another so that you may be healed. The effective prayer of a righteous man can accomplish much" (James 5:16 NASB). If you need deliverance in a certain area of temptation, then you should find a deliverance ministry to help you.

Sin Redefined

The Old Covenant defined sin as *doing* something wrong, but the New Covenant holds us to a higher standard. Now a person can commit sin by merely *wanting* to sin. Jesus described it in the Sermon on the Mount by saying:

> You're familiar with the command to the ancients, "Do not murder." I'm telling you that anyone who is so much as angry with a brother or sister is guilty of murder. ... You know the next commandment pretty well, too: "Don't go to bed with another's spouse." But don't think you've preserved your virtue simply by staying out of bed. Your heart can be corrupted by lust even quicker than your body. Those leering looks you think nobody notices — they also corrupt (Matthew 5:21,22,27,28 MSG).

Whether you call it "leering looks" as *The Message* paraphrases or "lust after" as the King James states, when you desire a man or woman sexually, you sin just as surely as if you had intercourse. You do not have to fantasize about having sex, masturbate, or even flirt with someone to dishonor your wife or husband and be guilty of the sin of adultery ... all you have to do, is *want to do it.*

> **Let's Get One Thing Straight**
> **TEMPTATION IS *NOT* SIN!**
> **Jesus was tempted yet *never* sinned.**

In a culture that promotes sexiness in women, men have opportunities to be tempted in every direction they turn. So, you might wonder: when does temptation becomes sin? James, the brother of Jesus, described it like this:

> *But each one is tempted when he is carried away and enticed by his own lust. Then when lust has conceived, it gives birth to sin; and when sin is accomplished, it brings forth death* (James 1:14,15 NASB).

To put it another way, I (Henry) once asked my friend, Peter Lord, a pastor in Titusville, Florida, about lust and he described it this way, "You know that I live in a state where women do a lot of sunbathing. So, let's say that I am jogging along one day and come upon an attractive woman sunning herself in her front yard wearing nothing but a string bikini and I glance over at her. Have I sinned? The answer is no, not unless I jog around the block to get another look." Temptation becomes sin when you take the next step, whatever that may be.

The words "lust" and "passion," apply not only to sex. You can sin by lusting for a car: a Lamborghini, Ferrari, or even a beat-up old Dodge Colt. It is not the thing that determines if it is lust, but the obsessive craving for something you don't have. This is not the same as liking something and purchasing it or even setting a goal to own it someday. Sin steps through the door when liking turns into compulsive craving ... craving becomes envy ... and envy morphs into jealousy.

WOMEN ONLY

Our materialistic culture purposely provokes desire, jealousy, and envy in women to motivate them to buy products which claim to make them become more attractive. Before you spend your money on 'stuff' consider God's advice for becoming the ideal woman:

What matters is not your outer appearance — the styling of your hair, the jewelry you wear, the cut of your clothes — but your inner disposition. Cultivate inner beauty, the gentle, gracious kind that God delights in. The holy women of old were beautiful before God that way, and were good, loyal wives to their husbands (1 Peter 3:3-5 MSG, emphasis added).

All women have been made in the image of God, and each one is beautiful in her own way — uniquely lovely, specially gifted, and distinctively talented. Women (and men, too) should fight the need to compare themselves to someone else. Paul warns in II Corinthians 10:12 that comparing is unwise.

You have probably heard that "beauty is in the eye of the beholder." That is true. In America, we call women beautiful who are skinny, tall, and big-bosomed with slender waists and a pleasing face. Some men in Russia, however, would describe a beautiful woman as one who weighs about 300 pounds and is strong enough to pick up 100 pound bag of potatoes and carry it out of the field. In China, many judge a woman's beauty by the size of her feet: the smaller the more beautiful. In Sri Lanka, a woman's beauty is based on the length of her neck. Some places in Africa rate a woman's beauty by how many children she can bear. Beauty truly is in the eyes of the beholder. You are one-of-a kind, unique individual incomparable to every other woman!

Top 8 Temptations Most Men and Some Women Face

1. Temptation to collapse under pressure

Some in our culture believe that it is acceptable to quit when the going gets tough. However, when your destiny is at stake, you cannot afford to concede defeat — even when holding on seems impossible.

Sometimes the price of giving up is too high and we have to meet temptation bravely with death-defying resolve.

The Apostle Paul mentored the young pastor, Timothy, about a special crown for *finishers*:

> *I have fought the good fight, I have finished the course, I have kept the faith; in the future there is laid up for me the crown of righteousness, which the Lord, the righteous Judge, will award to me on that day; and not only to me, but also to all who have loved His appearing* (II Timothy 4:7-8 NASB).

Don't allow *anything* to cause you to miss *your* crown! The Bible tells us that the day is coming when our lives will be judged and we will need something to place at Jesus' feet. At that time, your crown will come in very handy.

I (Bart) recall playing in the Texas state football championship in the late 80's. During the third quarter, the hitting was hard, the weather brutally cold, and the other team was winning. We desperately needed a momentum-changing play. At that strategic moment, the coach called a pass play and I was to be the receiver. As I approached the line of scrimmage, I knew I had to make a great play or our team would cave and we would lose the game. As the only player on the field who had experience playing in a state championship game, I felt it was up to me.

The ball was snapped, I hurtled off the line of scrimmage, the quarter back through a good pass, and I caught the ball in full stride. As I ran across the field ... cut back toward the goal line ... and found a perfect opening between the two defensive backs. I sped up and broke free of my pursuers and sprinted toward the goal line as fast as I could. Out of the corner of my eye I watched the yard markers pass in a blur — 50, 40, 30 — and then it happened. I heard a pop that sounded to me like a gunshot, my right leg began to burn with excruciating pain, and I knew that I had torn the muscle in my thigh.

My head screamed, "STOP RUNNING!" but my heart said, "No way!" I had to 'finish' despite the pain. I continued toward the goal line and scored a 62-yard touchdown run that won the game. Even though no one would have faulted me for quitting, folding under the pain on my injury, I just could not give up. You, too, will have occasions when you have every right to quit, but if you hang in there, refuse to give up despite the difficulty, you will win!

2. Temptation to tolerate an unrestrained thought life

Those who allow their minds to run free live under the control of their souls. To allow the soul to lead is like the tail wagging the dog. A *finisher* must gain control of his mind. An undisciplined thought-life is not an option for Christians:

> So then, brethren, we are under obligation, not to the flesh, to live according to the flesh — for if you are living according to the flesh, you must die; but if by the Spirit you are putting to death the deeds of the body, you will live. For all who are being led by the Spirit of God, these are sons of God (Romans 8:12-14 NASB).

Continually immersing yourself in God's Word through frequent Bible reading, will force your mind to yield to the power of the Word which is "sharper than a two-edged sword dividing the soul (mind, will, emotions) and the spirit" (see Hebrews 4:12).

In the early 90's, I (Bart) began to strongly pursue the Lord. I decided to learn all I could about God, and to try to rid myself of the lustful thoughts that plagued me. I had heard that the Word of God washes you clean, so I decided to put it to the test by reading God's Word every day. For two months, I read daily until I had read the Bible from cover to cover. Then, because I was experiencing God's presence and a new understanding of the Word, I began listening to the Bible daily while working.

Doing construction work, made it possible for me to listen to the Bible as much as I wanted. After listening all the way through the Bible 40 times, I stopped counting. The results were amazing: strongholds were breaking, my mind was being transformed, and my heart was coming alive with the fire and purpose of God. I am proof that the Word truly can transform the reader (or listener). If it worked for me, it will work for you, too!

3. Temptation to give in to sexual enticement

Guys, sometime find themselves in challenging situation concerning sex with other men. It can be something as simple a guy thumbing through a girlie magazine saying, "Wow! Take a look at this chick." Because most Christian guys don't want others to think they are standoffish, prudish, or a 'Bible thumper,' they take a peak.

However, Christian men do not need to give in to these situations. You can view temptation as an *opportunity* to strengthen yourself. You can say something like, "I don't need that." If you don't rule over these situations, they will roll over you. So get aggressive, speak their language (but without the vulgarity).

4. Temptation to avoid obedience because you do not want to give up authority over your life

The belief that I (Bart) should have the final say in my future kept me out of ministry for many years. I knew at an early age that I was called to ministry, but I became angry with God for choosing *me* without asking me what *I* wanted. Being raised in a pastor's home, I grew up in church and saw the 'dark side' of ministry, and I wanted no part of it.

As a little boy of four or five years-old, my father took me out in front of our house to show me the area where I was allowed to play. He pointed out the street's curb and instructed me, "Stay on the grass. Don't go near the curb." I promptly stepped up on the curb and began walking along it. My father spanked me and then repeated his warning. I, too, repeat myself by getting on the curb again for another stroll. The result was the same as before: a spanking. We continued in this way for four or five times until finally, instead of walking on the curb, I crossed the curb and sat down in the street. (And you thought *your* kids were strong-willed.)

My issue with human and godly authority was obviously rebellion, and it took years for me to fully understand and deal with it. Sometimes we downplay rebellion in our children (and ourselves) and even try to spin it into something positive by calling it persistence, tenacity, or perseverance. Yet, the penalty for rebellion against God can be a stiff one as King Saul learned when he disregarded God's orders and did things his own way. The prophet Samuel confronted him to say:

> ... **Rebellion is as the sin of divination**, and insubordination is as iniquity and idolatry. Because you have rejected the word of the LORD, He has also rejected you from being king (1 Samuel 15:23 NASB, emphasis added).

5. <u>Temptation to make yourself the standard against which you judge others</u>
This needs little explanation. Most of us see ourselves as 'normal' and gauge everything and everyone else by how they measure up to us. Paul, however, advises us to *get real*:

> ... *Don't be impressed with yourself. Don't compare yourself with others* (Galatians 6:4 MSG).

WOMEN ONLY
Do you ever walk into a room and inspect all the other women — their clothing, hair, make up, behavior, and other qualities — to weigh them against some ideal woman or the way you see yourself? The Bible encourages us to measure our selves against God's expectations and our faithfulness to fulfill our responsibilities, not against other people. Women with deep-seated feelings of inferiority may get satisfaction from playing the 'comparison game,' but eventually someone, will always outshine them and sparks feelings of insecurity.

6. <u>Temptation to lose control of your tongue in anger and to believe that expressing your feelings is your 'inalienable right'</u>
Most children and some adults need to learn that they do not have to say everything that comes into their mind. Jesus' plainspoken brother, James, shines light on this attitude with a blunt comment:

> If anyone thinks himself to be religious, and yet does not bridle his tongue but deceives his own heart, this man's religion is worthless (James 1:26 NASB).

WOMEN ONLY

Women (and some men) must be careful concerning gossip. The feminine need for social contact generates a weakness for some in this area. God created women to express themselves verbally and to think aloud. Consequently, some need take care not to fall into the sin of gossip.

I (Henry) have seen prayer and intercessory groups fall into the gossip trap. While discussing an issue and expressing themselves, they can break confidences and criticize people instead of simply taking the issues to God.

7. Temptation to believe that money produces happiness

Make no mistake; money can bring pleasure and produce moments of happiness and even bliss. However, neither money nor its pursuit can bring the life of joy we crave.

In recent years, the Church has learned again that God does indeed want his people to prosper. Yet, He wants to give us far more than a financial blessing. Consequently, the subject of prosperity receives only passing attention in Scripture. Jesus, our role model for Christian living, never displayed the trappings of wealth or taught the importance of getting rich. Jesus did, however, model something very important — a life of power and influence — a lifestyle that He announced we should also live:

... Go, preach, saying, "The kingdom of heaven is at hand."
Heal the sick, raise the dead, cleanse the lepers, and cast out
demons. Freely you received, freely give. (Matthew 10:7
NASB).

Insecure men and women with low self-esteem may believe that a lot of money will give them value and significance. Yet, only God can show us how important we are; money can never do that.

I (Henry) remember the day my wife and I received news that her father, who had been wealthy enough to retire at 42-years-old, had lost all the money he had saved and invested. I went to talk to him about his loss. He said to me, "I was going to leave that money to my ten children, but that God knows best." Although he had amassed a considerable fortune, his money didn't own *him*.

WOMEN ONLY

Some people base their happiness on the lifestyle made possible by wealth. Others have the 'shopping gene' and need to have the 'latest and greatest' to feel good about themselves. Women who do not have a secure place in their hearts toward their husbands or God, believe that money provides that security, but it never works. Jesus said that life isn't about having an abundance of things: "...Take care, and be on your guard against all covetousness, for one's life does not consist in the abundance of his possessions" (Luke 12:15 ESV, emphasis added).

8. Temptation to live in isolation from others

Our fast-paced, highly mobile, competitive culture does not offer many opportunities for Christian men to connect with their brothers. Yet, despite all our excuses, the real reason many men do not seek more interaction with other men is because deep down we do not like ourselves. And, we fear that if others get to know us, they will not like us either. However, every man needs at *least one* good friend; a person he can reach out to at any time, about any thing. God intended for us to have *many* men involved in our lives, true friends to whom we can admit our worst sin without fearing they will turn away from us.

WOMEN ONLY

Some of men's temptations come out of an over-confident ego, but the temptations some women face come from self-loathing. According to Mary Ellen Ashcroft, the author of Temptations Women Face: Honest Talk About Jealousy, Anger, Sex, Money, Food, Pride, many women are tempted to …

Fill their lives with 'stuff' — the temptation based on the mistaken belief that satisfaction can be found and controlled by having and getting 'things.'

Fill their lives with the trivial — this is the Martha mentality (see Luke 10:38-42). The temptation to keep yourself busy doing good things but never asking God if they are what He considers important, the things that really deserve your time and efforts.

Let anger consume them — anger itself isn't the temptation, but what comes along with it: (1) Failing to deal with the reason for antagonism (2) Saying or doing the wrong things in anger (3) Nursing anger until it become bitterness and hatred.

Focus on food or dieting — the temptation either to overeat to indulge the desire of the flesh, called "gluttony," or under-eat to find satisfaction in having a beautiful body rather than finding satisfaction in your relationship with Christ. This is a dead-end street because there is always someone who looks better and has more self-discipline.

Believe distortions about marriage — the temptation to believe that your relationship with a man is the answer to your deepest desires and needs. It can lead to investing more faith in romance than in God. Some women have discovered there is something worse than not having a man in their life, and that is having the wrong man.

Believe falsehoods about sex — the temptation to believe that a woman who has and enjoys sex with her husband is a whore, and she who abstains or doesn't enjoy it is a saint. It is also the temptation to exploit sex to gain a feeling of self-worth and satisfaction by using it to control her husband.

Get stuck in their dissatisfaction — dissatisfaction isn't the temptation rather what it creates — the sin of envy. Envy comes from believing that you are a victim because you are without what you think you need in life. Then, when you see someone who has the 'things' you believe would make you happy, you feel greed, jealousy, and envy.

Each of these temptations requires a renewing of the mind to the truth and a level of inner healing.

Little-known Facts About Temptation

- Temptation is the "breath of satan." Giving in to temptation is more than just surrendering to the "lust of the flesh," the "lust of the eyes," or the "pride of life"; it is opening yourself to the same smooth-talking liar who suckered the first two people into sinning. Christians who allowed themselves to yield to seeming 'harmless' temptations will awake one day to find they moved farther from God faster than they thought possible.

I, (Bart) had a memorable experience with temptation, and learned how serious God is about our obedience. During a business trip my new business partner asked me to take him 'out on the town.' This meant that I was supposed to take him to bars for a night of drinking and partying and foot the bill. Reluctantly, I agreed although I felt a 'check in my heart' about it. When I stepped out of my car and was walking toward the door, the Holy Spirit spoke in a voice that seemed audible as I touched the door handle saying, "Don't go in" ..."Don't go in."

When I looked over my shoulder to see who was speaking to me, no one was there. I paused and looked around for a few moments to shake off the feeling but went in the door. As I crossed the threshold, I felt the Spirit of God depart from me, and it felt as if someone poured ice water down my back. That man was one of the worst partners I ever had; every project we worked on was difficult. When he left 18 months later, I was glad to see him go. It took years for the Spirit of God to return to me in the same measure I had it before.

- Turn temptation into a positive by focusing on the opportunity it offers. Whatever you exercise grows stronger, muscles grow bigger and more powerful, and spiritual integrity works the same way. Exercising your character strengthens it, and it becomes easier to do the 'right thing.' But beware; the flip side is also true. Our faults also become stronger with exercise. Continual giving in to sin will cause a transgression to go from a weakness to a demonized stronghold of the enemy.

- Do not, however, become arrogant when you overcome temptation or make the mistake of thinking that you are strong enough to stand against it in your *own* power. Some temptations are so forceful they can crush you without God's help to withstand them. Fortunately, God has a strategy that will save you. Every temptation has a built-in escape hatch. The *Amplified Bible* probably explains this best:

    For no temptation (no trial regarded as enticing to sin), [no matter how it comes or where it leads] has overtaken you and laid hold on you that is not common to man .... But God is faithful [to His Word and to His compassionate nature], and He [can be trusted] not to let you be tempted and tried and assayed beyond your ability and strength of resistance and power to endure, but with the temptation **He will [always] also provide the way out** *(the means of escape to a landing place), that you may be capable and strong and powerful to bear up under it patiently* (I Corinthians 10:13, emphasis added).

Beware: you can race past God's exit from your temptation if fear is blinding you. So keep the eyes of your faith wide open for the means of escape. Some men have cried out to God for help but missed their last opportunity to exit because they did not like the way out that God provided, and drove off the cliff.

What To Do When You Are Tempted
A. **Call it what it is** — Don't fail to recognize it ... don't fake it ... don't pretend that it is something other than temptation!
B. **Call upon God for help** — By admitting that you have encountered temptation and by calling out to God for help, you expose the *deception of the temptation*. For example: a beautiful woman flirting with a man can be flattering but flattery is only a disguise for what is *really* happening — temptation!
C. **Call out for accountability** — Ask a Christian brother, your pastor or your wife to help by holding you accountable for your response to temptation.
D. **Call for deliverance** — If you think the temptation is rooted in a stronghold, then get help from someone who knows how to break demonic strongholds. A *stronghold* is "a lie that you have believed about

yourself, God, or someone else." Because you believe the lie, you treat it as the truth. One confirmation that you are dealing with a stronghold is that you cannot override it with your will. The human will can fail to do its job for several reasons:

- You really do not want to overpower the temptation for some reason.
- You believe that you cannot overcome the lie because you have tried and failed.
- You have accepted the lie so often that you have given up.

E. **Recall that you are not facing temptation alone** — During your temptation continually remind yourself that …
1. God is greater than any temptation you can have.
2. He has promised to provide you a way of escape.
3. He will come to your rescue.

F. **Call on God's Word to prepare you for future victories** — Strengthen and prepare yourself for your next go around with a temptation through the Scriptures:
1. Follow the advice God gave to Joshua for success, read God's Word:
   This Book of the Law shall not depart out of your mouth, but you shall meditate on it day and night, that you may observe and do according to all that is written in it. For then you shall make your way prosperous, and then you shall deal wisely and have good success (Joshua 1:8 AMP).
2. Pay special attention to scriptures about overcoming and avoiding particular kinds of temptation in the future.
3. Take Paul's recommendation to not only flee temptation, but to go after righteousness, faith, love, and peace:
   *So flee youthful passions and **pursue righteousness, faith, love, and peace**, along with those who call on the Lord from a pure heart* (2 Timothy 2:22 ESV).
4. Adopt King David's suggestion for cutting back on the number of temptations you face. *The Message* Bible paraphrases Psalms 1:1-6 in an unusual but practical way:
   … Don't hang out at Sin Saloon … don't slink along Dead-End Road … don't go to Smart-Mouth College. Instead, you thrill to

GOD's Word, you chew on Scripture day and night. You're a tree replanted in Eden, bearing fresh fruit every month, never dropping a leaf, always in blossom. You're not at all like the wicked, who are mere windblown dust — without defense in court, unfit company for innocent people. GOD charts the road you take. The road they take is Skid Row.

Action Steps

1. If you learn to lengthen your *moment of choice* and become more aware of the who, what, when, where, and how of your temptation, you have more time to recognize what is happening and thus do the right thing. Over the next two weeks make a record of every time you are tempted (make a written note). Note the '4-Ws and H,' and pay special attention to the *type* of temptation. Use the 8 categories given in this chapter (or add to them as needed). You may be surprised to discover that you are being tempted in only two or three areas.

2. After journaling your temptations ...
    a. Analyze them for what they have in common.
    b. Look for practical steps to take to avoid temptation. For example: you may discover that you are often tempted when you are with certain people or go to certain places.
    c. Based on your findings list the concrete actions you are going to take to avoid future temptations.

3. Ask the Lord to show you "hidden sins," temptations that you regularly give in to but have hidden from yourself.

4. If you do not have a close male friend, ask the Lord to bring a Christian guy into your life. Begin looking for that person and when you find a candidate, make the effort and invest the time required to develop a friendship. (The Bible says if you want to have friends, you must "show yourself friendly.") Create a goal to make at least one male friend over the next three months.

5. Each day schedule personal time with God — this is a must — like food to eat or air to breath. You need a daily quiet time with the Lord to finish strong.

In the next chapter ...
We talk about a part of you that is so important you can never become the man or woman God intended until you conquer it. The vital piece of real estate you must rule is the kingdom of your heart.

5

Chapter 5
Conquer the Kingdom of Your Heart

Whether you are the CEO of a Fortune 500 company or a stay-at-home mom ... a mature person or a teen ... a college professor or high school dropout, every man and woman has a kingdom to conquer — the kingdom of his or her heart.

> *He who has no rule over his own spirit is like a city that is broken down and without walls* (Proverbs 25:28 AMP).

To live the life for which you were created, fulfill your purpose and calling, and enjoy the abundant or 'maximized' life Jesus promised to believers, *you must win the war for your heart!*

The wise man, Solomon, confided the secret to maximized manhood and womanhood in Proverbs 4:23: *"Watch over your heart with all diligence, for from it flows the springs of life"* (NASB). Our hearts are like the wells that Abraham dug to water his flocks as he moved all around the area that would one day belong to his descendents. Those wells yielded life-giving water to his herd; yet, when he returned to use them again, he discovered that his enemies had stopped them up. The wells of a person's heart can become clogged with boulders of offense, judgments, and manipulation.

These internal boulders restrict the flow of *life* in our hearts and cause stagnation, because they are S-I-N. However, we can fail to recognize them as sin because they are often painful wounds of the soul. Even though, in many cases, we were innocent victims, still our wounds cause us to sin, and that *always* brings a death of some kind into our lives! So, dealing with our *issues* is not optional for Christians.

I (Henry) once ministered to a man who was unsuccessful in every area of life. He did not understand that a person cannot break God's law without creating consequences — even if you were the victim. His father had rejected and abused him throughout his childhood; consequently, he hated and refused to forgive him, and justified unforgiveness by saying that his father never admitted to being wrong. His unforgiveness closed off his heart to others, and he began to create all kinds of offense with other men and women including his family and friends. I was finally able to convince him that he must forgive his father to become a prosperous and successful man. With God's help, this man was able to release his father from the debt created by abusive actions. When his heart was freed of those boulders, he was able to recover his rightful inheritance of blessing and prosperity.

WOMEN ONLY

Offenses … judgments … and manipulation are familiar areas to both men and women because they come out of relationships. A good way to deal with the offenses and judgments of others is to follow a simple rule: "Don't take the offense personally." Easy to say but it will require effort.

Here is how it works — when someone says or does something belittling or insulting recognize that you are being offered a toxic brew to drink and mentally say, "No, thank you." You would not drink a cup of arsenic if it were offered to you, so why internalize an offense which is poison to your soul? Since you cannot control what others say and do, the best way to handle offense is to refuse to personalize it, to take ownership of it.

There is a difference between judging someone, being judgmental, and making **bitterroot judgments**. Bitterroot judgments poison your heart and distort your worldview. They create self-imposed boundaries that are illusory but seem so real they become a prison. These judgments are lies that deceive us about ourselves, our God, our world, and the people in it. They keep us from reaching our full potential and enjoying the satisfaction of becoming all God intended.

I (Henry) made a bitterroot judgment against my father. My dad cursed me in my mother's womb and refused to have anything to do with me as a child. My judgment against him was: "My father doesn't love or take ownership of me." Unconsciously, I extended this judgment to Father God. Consequently, for years I could not believe that He loved me for who I am. I believed His love was "performance based" and conditional. And, as with my earthly father, I could never quite measure up to His requirements. It was only after I dealt with the bitterroot judgment against my earthly father that I could feel loved by my heavenly Father. Ask the Lord to show you lies that you have believed because of bitterroot judgments. Every aspect of your life that is problematic or not flourishing is probably being influenced by a bitterroot judgment.

Manipulation, whether used *by* you or *on* you, is:
1. A way to compensate for an imagined personal weakness.
2. A feeling of inadequacy and incompetence.
3. The fear of being unable to get your needs fulfilled.

Although manipulation seems to come out of a mind-set of superiority or entitlement, at its root are *always* feelings of inferiority. If you are guilty of manipulation, begin believing that, with God's help, you are powerful enough to meet all your needs. Our weaknesses are God's opportunity to show Himself strong in our behalf; the Lord wants to be your strength. After all, each of us has a right to declare alongside Paul: *"I can do everything through him who gives me strength"* (Philippians 4:13 NIV).

If you are the one being manipulated, ask God for the courage to stop playing the victim, and say a polite but firm, "No!" to your manipulator.

Boulders of Unforgiveness
The most common sin in the lives of nearly every man and woman is not cheating, lying, stealing, adultery, or even pornography; it is *unforgiveness*.

While many would never allow themselves to indulge in more blatant sins, the pain of a wounded heart, and our perceived innocence, can seem to justify holding a grudge. However, forgiving is so important that Jesus clearly warned, "... *If you do not forgive, neither will your Father who is in heaven forgive your transgressions*" (Mark 11:26 NASB). Consider the cost of unforgiveness and make a decision to forgive those who have offended you.

There are often two penalties for unforgiveness, as for many other sins — a *moral penalty* and a *spiritual penalty*. The spiritual penalty is what we receive from God for our sin, and the moral penalty is what we reap naturally from sinning. As an illustration: let's say that your five-year-old son is playing in the yard and begins to climb a tree. You put your head out the backdoor and tell him not to do that until you can help him, and you then warn him that, if he doesn't stop, "He is in trouble!" Moments later, you hear him screaming in pain and rush outside to discover that, he tried to climb the tree without you, fell, and broke his arm. You rush him to the emergency room; en route, he pleads, "Dad please don't spank me. I know I did wrong." You respond, "I forgive you and I hope that you've learned a lesson." Your forgiveness is like releasing him from the *spiritual penalty* of disobedience. Yet, after the bone is reset, your forgiveness will not relieve him of the pain and inconvenience of a broken arm, that corresponds to the *moral penalty* for sin.

Peter must have been shocked with Jesus' answer about how often to forgive a person who sins against you (see Matthew 18:21-35). In these times, the rabbis taught that one must forgive as many as four times a day anyone who offended them. So, Peter must have felt especially spiritual by suggesting seven times daily and was no doubt astonished when Jesus said that he must forgive, not seven times, but 70 X 7 (490) times a day. Let's break that down to see what Jesus really meant:
> Most people have about 16 waking hours a day
> 16 hrs x 60 min/hour = 960 minutes
> 960 min divided by the 490 times Jesus said to forgive = forgiving every 1.95 minutes

In other words, Jesus was saying that we have to forgive continuously when offended. (Some Bible scholars believe that Jesus said 7 X 7, or 49 times, which gives a person about 20 minutes to maintain unforgiveness before they are required to forgive.) Either way we can deduce that it must be immediate and that *God expects us to live a lifestyle of forgiveness.*

Jesus continued this teaching with the parable of the king who forgave the debt of a servant who owed him 10,000 talents (about $40 million today). The forgiven man then demanded his money from someone who owed him only 100 denarii (about $20). When his debtor was unable to pay, the man who had been forgiven *much* put the man who owed him *little* into prison. The king heard about this and put the ungrateful servant into prison and declared that he would be tormented until he paid his debt. Then, to make certain that we did not miss the meaning of the story — forgiveness is not optional — Jesus explained:

> *"And that's exactly what my Father in heaven is going to do to each one of you who doesn't forgive unconditionally anyone who asks for mercy"* (Matthew 18:35 MSG).

It is easy for us to be like the ungrateful servant and forget how undeserving we are of the Lord's taking to the Cross our huge debt of sin; we can even take for granted His continuing forgiveness of our daily errors, and fail to forgive those who sin against us. The issue of 'on-going forgiveness' is so very important that Jesus put it at the beginning of the Lord's Prayer: *"... Forgive us our debts, as we also have forgiven our debtors"* (Matthew 6:12 NASB).

You have only two choices about forgiveness: you can obey and follow the teaching of Scripture or disobey and become bitter. Failure to forgive will create a bitterness that not only poisons *you* but ends up defiling the lives of everyone around you.

WOMEN ONLY
According to Dr. Katherine Piderman, the staff chaplain at the Mayo Clinic in Rochester, Minnesota, forgiveness is the act of untying yourself from thoughts and feelings that bind you to an offense committed against you. Forgiveness reduces the power those feelings have over you and can even ultimately lead to understanding, empathy, and compassion for the one who hurt you.

The doctor says that research indicates that forgiveness has many verifiable health benefits, such as:

Lower blood pressure
Stress reduction
Less hostility
Better anger-management skills
Lower heart rate
Lower risk of alcohol or substance abuse
Fewer depression symptoms
Fewer anxiety symptoms
Reduction in chronic pain
More friendships
Healthier relationships
Greater religious or spiritual well-being
Improved psychological well-being

She suggests that we deal with an offense early, before it balloons and we become swallowed up by bitterness or a sense of injustice.

Battle of the Brave Heart

"Wait!" you may be thinking, "I'm not holding unforgiveness." Or you might dismiss this teaching with a shrug and say, "I've already dealt with all that." However, this is so vitally important we must ask you to re-examine yourself and see if you have in fact dealt with *all* of your offenses.

What about:

The issues that caused you to leave a church abruptly?
The driver who recently put your life at risk by cutting you off in traffic?
That former girlfriend or boyfriend, ex-husband or ex-wife who wronged you?
The family member you refuse to be with during the holidays?
The person whose mission in life seems to be to humiliate you, particularly in front of others?

Your abusive boss and his unrealistic expectations?
Your father who was aloof or too busy to be a *real* Dad to you?
The mother who was so self-absorbed she didn't have time for you or your needs?
The son or daughter who has disappointed you?
The spouse who had an affair?

The possibilities for offense are endless, but perhaps those listed have reminded you of a wounded place that remains in your heart. Isn't it time for you to bravely come out of denial, pain, and sin? The procedure for getting free is simple, but the execution of it requires God's help:

1. Beg God to forgive you for the sin of withholding forgiveness and ask him to help you with the next step.
2. Totally, wholly forgive those who have sinned against you, in the same way as God has completely forgiven you.

Have you discovered that merely saying the words "I forgive you," often isn't enough? Perhaps you have heard the expression "Choose to forgive." Choosing to forgive is important but if we go no further, we've made forgiveness only a mental thing. Jesus taught that we must forgive from our hearts to satisfy God. That means giving up all the 'stuff' the other person caused — the pain, the anger, the wound, and any judgments you made because of the offense. If that sounds like God is asking too much, then consider that He removed even the knowledge of *our sin* from Himself "as far as the east is from the west" (see Psalms 103:12).

Offenses that are not plucked out, develop roots of bitterness that spread throughout the heart. Remember, the Bible teaches that "the issues of life" flow out of your heart and, if an offense is ignored or, worse yet, relived time after time, it will create a "bitterroot" that will defile your *whole heart*.

Looking carefully lest anyone fall short of the grace of God; lest any root of bitterness springing up cause trouble, and by this many become defiled (Hebrews 12:15 NKJV)

Offenses spread like an aggressive cancer corrupting all they touch. If you have met a bitter person, one who can find little that is good about anything, you have seen a person whose heart is poisoned by offense. Look well into their frowning face, because it could become a reflection of your own *unless* you choose to eradicate bitterroots caused by unforgiveness.

Perhaps the worst part of unforgiveness is not the bitter person we create of ourselves, but what we do to the lives of our children who learn through example that unforgiveness and bitterness is acceptable behavior. Sometimes our offenders may not know or care that they wounded us, but that does not matter. We forgive primarily for ourselves and for our children. *Let yourself out of jail!* In Jesus' parable, He was saying that if we fail to forgive, *we* will be imprisoned and tormented. Extending forgiveness is *your* 'get out of jail free' pass, not your offender's.

I (Henry) ministered to a young woman who said she had forgiven her family for all the wounds they had given her; however, she never really let go of her offenses. She continually found fault with one family member or another, especially her mother. Over-taken by deep depression, she medicated herself with drugs and alcohol. She eventually stopped using illegal drugs but still took prescription medicine to control her depression. She was never able to reconcile with her family. She told me, "I have forgiven them, but I need to keep my distance because they continue to hurt me." She found herself alone, all because she refused to consider that *real* forgiveness is more than mere words.

There resides within many of us a *Secret Person of the Heart.* That is the person we *really* are. It is 'secret' because we hide them from everyone, *even* our conscious mind. We who have experienced pain in life (and who hasn't) usually bury it, and project to the outside world a *personality* we think will help us to find the love and acceptance we desperately want. We can begin to believe that we actually are the personality we constructed and forget the real us, the Secret Person of our heart.

Yet, the wounds we bury and hide from our conscious mind are like corpses pushed underwater that will sooner or later re-emerge. One way we can know that we have a 'floater' is when we over-respond and surprise ourselves with the depth of our emotional response over something relatively minor. Another way to know that buried pain is surfacing is if we experience deep sadness, uncontrollable crying, laughing, or anger over things that do not merit such powerful reactions. This occurs when relatively mild events put us in touch with forgotten pain. If this has happened to you, or you believe that you may have unresolved issues, you should do two things:

1. Ask God to reveal your hidden wounds so that you can allow Him to heal the hidden pains of your heart.
2. Get help from a ministry like Elijah House Ministries that can lead you to inner healing.

How to Know When You Have *Not* Forgiven

You have *not* forgiven if you …

1. *Insist that the offenders realize how deeply they hurt you.* Actually, you are withholding forgiveness until they apologize for the pain they caused.
2. *Warn them, "I forgive you this time, but you better not do it again!"* This is putting the offender on probation, not offering forgiveness.
3. *Declare, "I will never let that happen to me again."* You are protecting a heart wound and you will not allow anyone, including God, into that painful area.
4. *Say, "I forgive you, but I don't want to have anything to do with you ever again!"* You really mean, "I don't forgive you. I reject and separate myself from you so you can't hurt me again."

There is a big difference between giving *forgiveness* and restoring lost *trust*. Forgiving is *not* pretending that nothing happened. The wounded person must understand that forgiving is not the same as re-establishing trust. Rather, forgiveness is removing the debt the other created by the wrong (or sin) they committed. *Trust must be earned; it cannot be restored by forgiveness alone.* Although broken trust can certainly be mended over time, it often leaves a fading but lasting scar on a relationship.

WOMEN ONLY
The person who many women and, for that matter, men have the greatest difficulty forgiving is an ex-spouse who failed to meet their expectations.

However, we can have unrealistic expectations of marriage. Some women have looked for a husband to give them the affirmation they never received from their father. Others may expect their husband to be Prince Charming, the guy who will facilitate the childish fantasy of "living happily ever after."

Some guys marry to find a replacement for an over-attentive mother; others are looking for the perfect sex-machine, and so on. Everyone who marries to get a 'need' met has set themselves up for disappointment.

The only kind of marriage relationship that really works is one based on real love. The Amplified Version of Ephesians 5:33 explains it like this:

... Let each man of you [without exception] love his wife as [being in a sense] his very own self; and let the wife see that she respects {and} reverences her husband [that she notices him, regards him, honors him, prefers him, venerates, and esteems him; and that she defers to him, praises him, and loves and admires him exceedingly].

Read through God's formula for a successful marriage (above) again but this time, instead of looking for your former (or present) spouse's shortcomings, study the text carefully to determine where you fail to be the mate He needs for you to be. There are no verses in the Bible that relieve us from being a good husband or wife, should our mate fail to be a good spouse. However, many discover that when they admit to and repent of their own shortcomings in marriage, they can find the grace to forgive their spouse's mistakes.

Discernment, Evaluation, and Judgment

Those who would win the battle for the kingdom of their hearts must become enforcers of the peace. They must root out and eliminating the conflicts that drown out the quiet voice of discernment.

Discernment is a gift that borrows from the Spirit of Revelation and Wisdom — one of the Seven Spirits of God mentioned in Revelation 3:1, 4:5, 5:6. Wisdom comes to us through the indwelling Holy Spirit Who also brings us peace. Peace is a vital factor to the free flow of wisdom and is the 'potting soil' for wisdom in our hearts.

Evaluation is to form an opinion based on what can be learned *naturally* through our five senses and thinking. (Many of us evaluate a situation based upon previous experience and think of it as *discernment*.) Once an evaluation is made, it becomes a *judgment* that we consider 'fact.' However, we cannot come to a knowledge of the truth until we repudiate inaccurate 'facts,' (lies) that we have believed and used to reach incorrect conclusions. Human evaluations are often wrong, but the Spirit of Discernment is never mistaken.

The only way to know that we are operating in the Spirit of Discernment is by the Spirit of Truth. The Holy Spirit can tell us what spirit is influencing us — the Spirit of God, the human spirit, or an evil one. When someone speaks truth, it bears witness within us because the Holy Spirit residing in believers represents Jesus Who is "the way, the **truth,** and the life." The truth, when spoken, has the ring of authenticity.

The 'ring of truth' can be illustrated by the difference between the sound made by fine crystal and glass when they are struck. Although they may look the same, crystal 'rings' a sweet clear tone and glass merely sounds a 'ding.' Discernment has a 'right' sound but, evaluation or judgment may please the mind with a solid-sounding "ding," but it can never reverberate within our spirits. Part of maturity is learning to distinguish the difference between dings and rings.

I (Bart) have found that I can begin in *discernment* but end up in *evaluation,* if I allow other people's opinions to influence me. For example: I've been advised at times to confront a person concerning their wrong doing, yet what they really needed was love and help. Each of us needs to learn to use the Spirit of Discernment rather than evaluating from our natural mental abilities. To live in discernment rather than judgment, we have to live in 'The Garden' by spending time in prayer and intimacy with God, and eat from the Tree of Life by consuming His Word.

Another difference between the Spirit of Discernment and natural evaluation is that discernment operates without *foreknowledge*. Knowing something through the five senses can affect your evaluation and be mistaken for the Spirit of Discernment. A simple example would be a child who comes to you with a chocolate smear on his face, and you "know" he is lying when he denies getting eating forbidden candy bars. This kind of 'knowing,' although correct at times, is not supernatural but natural. We can be 95% right and only 5 % wrong and still make a bad decision.

You don't, however, need a Word of Knowledge or prophecy to discern how God feels about things you *already* know are right and wrong. God gave us a brain and expects us to use it. We learn that the stove is hot and can burn our hands and then use that knowledge to avoid getting burned again. (We don't need a prophetic word from God not to touch a hot stove or not to commit sin.) The Spirit of Wisdom and Discernment is of great value but not our only source for accurate information.

We also have the Bible, as well as people whom God has positioned to speak into our lives. Discernment will show us what is behind a matter: the source from which an issue flows. Our goal is to live in the Spirit of Revelation and Wisdom with the peace of God while operating with the mind of Christ, making good choices and acting wisely in every situation.

FOR WOMEN

Paul, in I Corinthian 2:14,16 says an astonishing thing; he declares that we can think like God, have the "Mind of Christ":

But a natural man does not accept the things of the Spirit of God, for they are foolishness to him; and he cannot understand them, because they are spiritually appraised. ...we have the mind of Christ (NKJV).

Having the "mind of Christ" is the reward for those women (and men) who conquer the kingdom of their minds. To get to that place, we must recognize the futility of operating out of the natural mind and begin processing life in the way we were created to function, through our spirits.

Adam and Eve were created with bodies and souls but lived with their human spirits constantly in contact with God, until they sinned. God desires this same level of intimacy with every born-again person. Those who would walk this earth with the same power and wisdom that Jesus demonstrated must return to a Garden of Eden-like relationship with God.

Action Steps

1. Prayer Points: *Dear Jesus, I understand that you are the Spirit of Wisdom and Revelation, and I ask You to fill my mind, will, and emotions to overflowing with Your thoughts, Your will, and Your emotions. I want to operate in the Spirit of Discernment, I want to know what is behind the issues of my life, and make good decisions that bring life to me and those around me. Amen.*

2. Examine, with God's help, your life for offenses (use pencil and paper to make notes). Look honestly at your relationships at home, at work, at church, and elsewhere and try to recall every occasion where people have wronged or hurt you. Look back over your childhood and consider the messages you received from your father and mother and other significant adults in your life. Ask yourself if they built you up, or put you down?

3. When you have exhausted your memories of every occasion when someone hurt you, ask the Holy Spirit to show you additional offenses that you have forgotten. (Do not ignore offenses that you believe are resolved.) Treat an incident that comes to mind, as if it needs further attention. Deep wounds are often many-layered, and each layer has issues that have to be dealt with independently. Now that you have a list of offenses:

    ✓ Ask God to forgive you for holding the offense and the sins it caused you to commit.

    ✓ Begin speaking forgiveness to each person *aloud* in prayer.

    ✓ Go to the people on your list (or phone them) and ask their forgiveness for any wrongdoing, or at least for holding an offense against them. (If that person is dead, then ask the Lord to deliver the message and believe He can resolve it.)

    ✓ Do not use your apology to cause the offender to feel shame for what they did or to try to get an apology.

✓ Truly forgive them, even if they do not believe they wronged you or they believe that *you* were to blame.

Pray this prayer of forgiveness:
Father I forgive (name) *from my heart for all the things* (he or she) *did to me.* (Now tell God everything they did and, when you finish the list, declare) *I let them go free; I lay nothing to their charge; I place them into your hands, Father for justice. I forgive them because you, Heavenly Father, have already forgiven me. I bless them; make me a blessing to them.*

Now visualize their offenses as IOUs written on pieces of paper and see yourself tearing the IOUs into confetti, as you release them with all your heart from their debt.

4. Look for opportunities to practice *discernment* rather than evaluation. Ask God to help you:
    1. Become more discerning about your personal relationships with your wife, children, and others.
    2. Be more discerning at work with your boss and co-workers.
    3. Move to a new level of discernment concerning spiritual things — in your gifts, anointings, and callings.

5. Go to a mirror, and declare this while looking yourself in the eye:
I am a discerning person; I make good decisions; I am full of Godly wisdom, and I have the mind of Christ. I will no longer hold onto old issues because I am free from my past and, from this day forward, I am free to apprehend the future and I to see great things ahead.

Repeat this declaration until it is firmly set in your heart and mind. (You might write it on a 3 x 5 card to carry with you until memorized.) Say it in the morning when you are preparing for the day, and again in the evening as before going to bed. In fact, you may want to use the mirror as a trigger and speak this prayer every time you see your reflection throughout the day.

In the next chapter ...
We get down to basics and discuss the key things God looks at when He evaluates you for promotion. Regardless of the past, this is your season to get the "right stuff" going on in your life and for you to shine!

Chapter 6
Knights in Shining Honor

God is calling men (and women) to shine with honor and integrity. Our radiance increases as our lives manifest more and more of God's righteousness:

> ...*The path of the righteous is like the light of dawn, that shines brighter and brighter until the full day* (Proverbs 4:18 NASB).

Since *righteousness* is not a word we often hear outside of church, it could be translated into contemporary language, as "character," which includes the concept of integrity. Without character and integrity, we cannot accomplish anything of lasting value or significance.
You can be only as good as your character allows!

To become all the Lord intended and operate effectively in our God-given purpose, we must become armored against attacks of the enemy on our integrity. Character is our armor and, if we have chinks in our armor (weaknesses), those are the places we are vulnerable to the satan's assault. Consequently, God wants to strengthen us in those areas. The armor of character is not the kind we put on or take off; rather, it develops from the inside out something like a callous. Character grows in us when we *do*, and continue doing, the *right thing* even should it becomes painful and costs us something we value.

To illustrate how the protection the armor of character works let me (Henry) give you an example: We have already mentioned that the ministry of Dr. Billy Graham is character-filled. Consequently, should someone bring an accusation against him, no one would believe them. They would think, "This does not sound like the godly man I know." When a person's character is strong and their armor is sure, it covers their back.

WOMEN ONLY

God expects everyone to be righteous or 'virtuous':
A capable, intelligent, {and} virtuous woman — who is he who can find her? She is far more precious than jewels {and} her value is far above rubies {or} pearls" Proverbs 31:10 AMP).

Do not, however, mistake 'virtuous' with its legalistic counterpart, "good girl." Well-meaning parents have made 'niceness' a Christian value for their daughters by teaching them that Jesus only likes "good girls," therefore they must repress their emotions and always act 'nice.'

Becoming a woman of virtue, however, begins with being real with yourself, with others, and with God. Be honest about your shortcomings, be transparent with others when it is appropriate, and confess your weaknesses to God to receive forgiveness and receive the strength to overcome them. Allow God to prune the branches of your life that fail to yield righteousness. John 15:2 says, "Every branch in Me that does not bear fruit, He takes away; and every {branch} that bears fruit, He prunes it so that it may bear more fruit" (NASB).

Mothers (along with fathers) have a responsibility for building character in their children. Fathers primarily impart worth, and mothers take the lead in nurturing and teaching character. Many women have also been able to help their husbands develop character merely by being a godly example.

Life Just Isn't Fair!

Men and women throughout the ages have bemoaned the fact that life is rarely fair. Job, who holds the all-time record for having undeserving things happen, lamented: *"Man, who is born of woman, is short-lived and full of turmoil"* (Job 14:1 NASB). To expect life always to be "fair" is naïve or living in denial. The unwelcome truth is: bad things *do* happen to good people, and they can and will happen to you and me. Yet, God reassures us in Romans 8:28, that He will make all things [even the bad stuff] work together for [our] good.

Some Christians have understood Scripture to say that a person of faith can live a trouble-free existence. Some have gone so far as to question the spirituality of anyone going through hard times. Jesus, however, was a realist and warned that we will have problems in this life, *but* we can have a good outcome through Him:

> ... *In the world you have tribulation and trials and distress and frustration; but be of good cheer [take courage; be confident, certain, undaunted]! For I have overcome the world. [I have deprived it of power to harm you and have conquered it for you.]* (John 16:33 AMP).

Overcoming requires us to fight our way through the problem with God's help. Remember:

- Daniel was delivered out of the lion's den but only after spending what must have seemed like a very long night with those fierce carnivores.
- The three Hebrew children were delivered from Nebuchadnezzar's fiery furnace, but they first had to walk through the flames.

Although many of our problems can be attributed to reaping the reward of bad actions and poor decisions, just living in a fallen world causes us to be exposed to difficulties. Jesus, however, empowers us to overcome *all* difficulties and enforce God's will upon the earth.

Our inevitable struggles play a very important part in our spiritual growth by either producing character or exposing the lack of it. Character is generated when we refuse to take the easy way out, resist internal and external pressures, and do what is right regardless of the costs. A failure of integrity always results when we compromise to get relief from the pressures of our situations. God uses the problems of everyday life to produce His character in us. This is what Peter was referring to when he instruct, *"... As he who called you is holy, you also* **be holy in all your conduct***"* (1 Peter 1:15 ESV, emphasis added).

Our efforts to become righteous are like the struggles of the worm in a cocoon trying to break free to become a butterfly. Should he be cut free from the cocoon, he would be unable to fly. The same struggle that brings him freedom also develops the muscles as a butterfly needs to take wing. Our struggles are much the same; God delivers us from some things, but requires us to fight our way through others, so that we can emerge, like the butterfly, strong and capable of fulfilling our purpose.

WOMEN ONLY

Husbands should seek out their wives' encouragement during difficult times. When your guy goes through dark times, it is an opportunity to be there for him, "She comforts, encourages, {and} does him only good as long as there is life within her" (Proverbs 31:12 AMP). During tough times, God is forming and testing him. You can help by creating a place where he feels safe and does not have to be constantly on guard.

When I (Bart) was in my early 30's, I went through a very difficult purging time. One day I came home from the office and my wife, Kim, took one looked at me and said, "WOW! You must have had a day from hell." I looked her squarely in the eye and told her that everything had been taken from me but my birthday."

She embraced me and whispered in my ear, "I can tell this is very hard on you, and I am proud of the courage, stamina, wisdom, and strength that you are showing. I'm proud to be your wife." Nothing she said actually changed the circumstances, and she, too, would suffer the consequences of that day, but her encouragement and affirmation made a huge difference. By shining the light of her encouragement in my darkest moment, she helped me find my way back from the most devastating time of my life.

> A man needs to know that his wife will stand with him no matter what comes (or what goes); that she will be there without complaint or speculation about what he might have done differently. There are times when the thing a husband needs most from his wife is merely to be held and encouraged.

Roots of Rotten Character

We compromise our character to get what we want or to avoid what we fear. Compromise often results from a lack of faith in God's goodness, His good intentions toward us, and His ability to meet our needs, or because we do not want to give God control of our lives.

Take *lying* as an example — one recent study found that most people lie once or twice a day and, over the course of a week, the average person deceives about 30 people. Experts have found that people lie in order to …

1. Get their way
2. Elude confrontation
3. Shift blame
4. Save face

When we really come to believe that God is good, that He will actually meet *all* our needs, that *His approval* is more important than the approval of man (or our fears of rejection), we will find greater freedom to act with integrity. Solomon makes clear the results for acting righteously and the penalty if we don't:

> *The wicked earns deceptive* [fictitious] *wages, but one who sows righteousness gets a sure reward* (Proverbs 11:18 ESV).

The writer of the book of Romans goes even further and tells us not to lose heart in our difficulties, because it will produce good results in our life: *"… We rejoice in our sufferings, knowing that suffering produces endurance, and endurance produces character, and character produces hope"* (Romans 5:3-4 ESV).

WOMEN ONLY

The only good thing about bad character is — we aren't stuck with it. We can change it and become the virtuous person God intends us to be. No one is born either good or bad; our character is the result of choices we make. However, even bad decisions can be reversed; it is never too late to become a righteous person.

Women (or men) who long for self-esteem but are driven by a deep sense of inferiority, may engage in unhealthy relationships and indulge in unproductive fixations like: greed, envy, gluttony, laziness, anger, lust, and envy.

An obsession to 'be liked' or any other fixation can become the center of our life, replacing God on the throne of our heart. Sins are the symptoms of problems that lie in our heart. Once we truly make Jesus king of our heart, He will endeavor to heal us of erroneous beliefs and dysfunctional behavior. This, however, can occur only when we bring all of our needs and desires to the Cross and put them to death in sweet surrender to Him.

Immature, Inept, and Insensitive

The media often portrays men as childish, incompetent, and heavy-handed. Although exaggerated, this negative caricature unfortunately has some basis in truth. Even men who are skilled and successful at their jobs can be fumbling failures at home.

The world of work is a place where many men feel comfortable and knowledgeable; it is a situation for which they have been trained, feel confident and competent, understanding its boundaries and rules. Home, on the other hand, can be an alien (and even terrifying place) filled with people who act oddly and issues that can seem beyond comprehension. Many men do not grasp the motivations of their wives or their children; nor do they understand the dynamics of being a husband and father. Consequently, some men respond by becoming:

- *An Absentee* — *"Sorry, I have to work late"* — *Dad* who flees from problems at home by staying away, at work or other places, as much as possible.

- **A Passive** — *"Huh? I'm watching this show. Did you say something?"* — **Dad** who clutches his TV remote, ignoring his family.
- **A Dictator** — *"Do as I say; or #!#!#!#!"* — **Dad** who believes he must exert tyrannical control to play his part and may become heavy-handed doing it

Then again, some men operate from a child-like perspective of 'entitlement.' They still think of themselves as little boys who need their wives and children to cater to their needs in order to feel loved. Called by some the "Peter Pan Syndrome," such men thinks of themselves as little boys who are incapable of accepting adult responsibilities and often seek a mothering relationship with their mates. God, however, created men to be the other way around; a man is to care for his wife and children. "Peter Pan," thus creates a problem for a woman who desires a mature man for a husband, rather than a little boy.

I (Henry) think of these men as "frozen in time." Life to them is only about having fun and enjoying themselves, and they want their wives to be playmates or at least tolerant. They are never willing to shoulder the responsibilities of a *real* man: one who knows that he is called by God to be the leader of his home. These men are so preoccupied with themselves; they are often shocked when their wives eventually leave them. I once ministered to such a man. One Valentine's Day, he came home from work with a box of candy and flowers to discover a note from his wife posted on the refrigerator saying "I am gone, don't come looking for me. It is over." He was so occupied with having fun and enjoying life that he failed to notice the true state of his relationship with his wife.

WOMEN ONLY

If you are married to a "Peter Pan," do NOT become his playfellow or allow him to force you into the role of being his "mother." This will only make matters worse and ensure that he never changes. Instead of constantly rescuing him from the consequences of his childishness, you must allow him to experience the penalty of child-like decisions (or lack of making a decision) so he can learn the necessity of growing up.

There is hope, however, most men make changes very quickly when something no longer works for them. The "Peter Pan" husband will learn to grow up when his "pixie dust" loses its magic.

Character vs. Giftedness

The confusion about character and giftedness has caused some to reach mistaken conclusions about people: We've assumed that a person's level of giftedness and anointing signifies their degree of character and thought that having the ability to operate in spiritual gifts indicates righteousness.

Jesus made an helpful statement in Matthew 7:22,23 about spiritually gifted people. Speaking of Judgment Day He said:

> Many will say to Me on that day, "Lord, Lord, did we not prophesy in Your name, and in Your name cast out demons, and in Your name perform many miracles?" And then I will declare to them, "I never knew you; DEPART FROM ME, YOU WHO PRACTICE LAWLESSNESS" [unrighteousness] (NASB).

Can a person prophesy, cast out demons, and perform miracles and yet be un-righteous? Yes, we have to draw that conclusion from this scripture. Consequently, the Association of Bridge Churches, whose overseer is John Paul Jackson, with whom I [Bart] am aligned as a pastor, give greater value to character than giftedness.

Many have believed that the anointing to do a job qualifies a person for the position. Yet, consider David who, although anointed king as a young man, was not crowned for several decades. David had the gifts to rule, but he needed more: to become a soldier and leader of men. Most importantly, David had to become what Saul was not, a man of integrity — a knight in shining honor.

David needed to have his honor tested, time after time, and it had to be hardened in the fire of adversity … and so do we. First loved and then despised, by a king who eventually attempted to murder him. David had to flee and live the rough life of a hunted outlaw for many years. Even though it was in his heart to do the right thing, he had to *grow* in integrity. When David's character qualified him to be king, God promoted him into his destiny ... and the Lord is working with us in exactly the same way.

Everyday problem-solving forges our character as we practice becoming more righteous. Problems are the heat that brings our 'impurities' (areas of weak character) to the surface so that we can deal with them with God's help. He exposes the chinks in our armor so that we can be purified, strengthened, mended, and polished. Only then are we able to withstand the enemy's attacks upon our character that would otherwise destroy us, tear down the good we have done, and make it impossible for us to reach the pinnacle God intends for us.

WOMEN ONLY
Sometimes women have to cope with situations caused by their husband's bad decisions. I (Henry) had a friend who was a fine doctor. He believed that he had to make all the decisions for his family. His wife was usually in agreement with him, especially when times were good. However, he made one very bad decision which cost him his practice and sabotaged their financial future. His mistake made it impossible for her to continue living the life to which she had become accustomed. She became enraged with him for making that costly choice without giving her the right to be heard.

Should you find yourself in a similar position remember this, regardless what you may lose, no one can steal the most important thing — your destiny. Our Lord provides second, third, fourth, and innumerable chances.

Boot Camp for Champions
Have you ever felt that life was just *too* difficult ... that God was making things *too* hard for you ... or that He was stretching you beyond your breaking point? My (Bart's) mentor, John Paul Jackson, says:

Little battles produce little champions,
Big battles produce big champions.

The battles you fight, and the obstacles you overcome, define you. Little battles rarely seem small when we are experiencing them, because God tailors our battles to our ability to conquer them. Look at David's progression from shepherd boy to king. Consider the story of David and Goliath—how a young man with no training in combat was able to overcome a giant Philistine warrior who was considered undefeatable. Even though David was uncomfortable with a suit of armor and the weapons of war, God had prepared him to defeat this giant warrior. You may remember when David was reassuring Saul that he could win he mentioned the highlights of his resume:

> *Your servant has struck down both lions and bears, and this*
> *uncircumcised Philistine shall be like one of them, for he has defied the*
> *armies of the living God* (I Samuel 17:36).

This is how God works to prepare us for our battles: first the lion ... then the bear ... and finally the big scary giant. However, overcoming Goliath was not David's ultimate victory; God had nations for him to conquer. David was defined by the battles he fought and won. Each hurdle he jumped, each problem he overcame, led him closer to the crown. Eventually the day came when the leaders of Israel asked David, the boy who had bested a giant, to be their king.

David was more determined to be a man of integrity than he was to be king. Two times, God put Saul at David's mercy, and his associates begged him to kill Saul, but Dave refused to begin his reign by ending that of his predecessor. He could have so easily rationalized: "who would blame me for killing a man who is trying to kill *me*, and taking the crown from his head and placing it upon my own. After all, did not the prophet anoint *me* to be king?"

When *we* refuse to compromise in difficult times, we display a trustworthiness that makes it possible for God to promote us, and for our families and others to trust us. David understood how promotion works in God's Kingdom; he penned the words:

For not from the east nor from the west nor from the south come promotion and lifting up. But God is the Judge! He puts down one and lifts up another (Psalm 75:6,7 AMP).

WOMEN ONLY
In a culture where most women work and many hold important positions, a woman may be tempted to use her femininity to win favor. However, to do so is to usurp God's place as the Giver of favor. God not only declares that He is the one who promotes, but announced in Psalms 4:12 that He is the source for favor: "For it is You who blesses the righteous man [or woman], O LORD, You surround him with favor as with a shield" (NASB).

Allow God to do His job, in His timing; don't try to do it for Him. Those who do not wait on God for their promotion (men or women) and use manipulation (which the Bible says is like witchcraft) risk pushing the Lord out of their careers and thus create a stronghold for the enemy in their lives.

Cheating On Integrity

As Christians, we know that God expects us to be righteous in everything we say and do, and most Christians are obedient until it becomes inconvenient. When the pressure is on, we may be tempted to engineer circumstances so that we only *partially* obey God, while making it appear that we have been fully obedient.

When doing the 'right thing' requires more than we want to give (or give up) we can fudge a little ... lie a little ... or tell a partial truth. We conveniently forget there is One who always sees us and is never fooled:

"Can any hide himself in secret places that I shall not see him?" saith the LORD. "Do not I fill heaven and earth?"... (Jeremiah 23:24 KJV).

We may justify our actions by telling ourselves that we hurt no one else by what we do in secret. (Christian men who watch Internet porn often employ this rationalization.) Yet, to believe that our actions, even those that go unobserved, will have no consequences is merely a self-serving denial of truth. At the very least, our actions affect *us* to change how we interact with the people in our life.

What we do in secret reveals our true **character** ... our character reveals our **heart** ... our heart qualifies (or disqualifies) us for **promotion**, and *"... the Lord looks on the heart"* (I Samuel 16:7 NIV).

> **WOMEN ONLY**
> We can make the mistake of believing that God considers the 'good things' we do when He evaluates us for a promotion: volunteer activities, good deeds, the hours we spend in intercession, etc. While He certainly considers our obedience, we cannot buy promotion from the Lord with godly actions; promotion comes only from a righteous heart. Both men and women should ask themselves: What are the real motives behind the 'good things' I do? Am I trying to convince God or others that I am something more than I really am?

The Heart – the Key to Character

It would be great if we could instantly become people of integrity merely by deciding to do so. Although making that decision is an important beginning, most of us go through a process where we compromise our integrity less and less, and the things we compromise become of lesser importance.

Being a person of character is something we have to require of ourselves and make our way of life. We have to develop the resolve of Job concerning integrity and shout with him defiantly:

> *"I **will** maintain my righteousness and never let go of it; my conscience **will not** reproach me as long as I live"* (Job 27:6 NIV, emphasis added).

Although it seems logical to connect *being* righteous with *acting* righteous, it doesn't work that way. Change has to occur from the inside out rather than outside in. When righteousness becomes a condition of the heart, our actions reveal it:

A good man out of the good treasure of the heart brings out good things; and an evil man out of the evil treasure brings out evil things (Matthew 12:35 NKJV).

For *permanent* change to occur, we have to allow *God* to change our heart, He is the only One qualified and capable of performing this process. The first step is, of course, to become born-again, which allows God to reside within you through the Holy Spirit and to recreate your spirit as righteous. The Spirit of God then begins a campaign to convert the other areas of your heart to be righteous. This crusade only ends when every part of the soul is subject to the authority of the re-born human spirit.

To illustrate this point, I (Bart) will tell you about Allen Ray. Ray gave his heart to the Lord as a teenager; he felt called to the mission field but did not go, but instead went to college. During college, he became disillusioned with the Church, and his spiritual growth stopped for a time. Ray believed that abortion should be a woman's choice and that women should be able to terminate pregnancy for any reason. Growing up in the ghetto, he had seen the horrors of backstreet abortions and the dreadful treatment of unwanted children. So, he accepted abortion-on-demand as a better way.

However, a day came when Ray accompanied his teenage grandson to a church outreach at a local abortion clinic. The kids stood with red tape over their mouths silently praying that God would end abortion and save the lives of the unborn. As Ray stood there with them, he began to weep because he could hear unborn children crying out for help. They were not just calling to everyone; they were speaking to him specifically. They were repeatedly entreating him, "Ray, help us!" This experience completely changed Ray's opinion on abortion. Inward change is what we are talking about — real change always happens from the inside out.

When we come to understand the truth about who God is, and who we *really* are, our emotions can be tamed, and we can begin acting out of honor and integrity. How, you might ask, does God work to make our heart righteous? He 'squeezes' it to force out the toxic elements. This process not only *sounds* uncomfortable, it *is* and must be, to provide enough incentive for our mind, will, and emotions to expel the 'issues' at the root of our unrighteousness.

Because much of what we do is by habit or engrained response, we can retrain ourselves to righteousness by becoming more 'intentional' in our actions. That means, we become more aware of *what* we do and *why* we do it. One way to become more 'intentional' is to make an effort to be more tuned into the presence of the Holy Spirit, Who resides in each of us, throughout the day.

A Knight's Code

Boys often become fascinated by stories of King Arthur and the Knights of the Round Table. Most young boys have fought dragons, engaged evil villains in one-on-one combat, and saved damsels in distress, either in video games or during imaginary play. As fathers, we need to encourage that kind of activity because our sons are role-playing to become heroes: men of character and high ideals. Like knights during the Age of Chivalry, our lives must also be value-focused and character-driven. God grows character in us gradually, beginning in one area and working outward, until integrity becomes our lifestyle.

Righteousness refers to living within the boundaries that God established for mankind. Those boundaries are expressed in the Bible as a code of conduct for those men and women who want to live a *maximized life*. Obviously, our Creator knows best how we can enjoy the successful and exciting destiny He created for us. As we follow His ways, God has promised:

> *GOD's love ... is ever and always, eternally present to all who fear him, Making everything right for them and their children as they follow his Covenant ways and remember to do whatever he said* (Psalms 103:17-18 MSG).

Action Steps

1. If you are ready to begin the pursuit of righteousness or you want to renew your quest for character, then pray this prayer aloud:
   God, I want to be a person of integrity and character, please forgive me for the times I have fallen short. I know that I cannot obtain your approval through my effort, but, I need a change of heart. So, I ask you to create in me a clean heart and renew a right spirit in me" Please help me when I am being tempted to will make the right choices. I desire to be your knight in shining honor. Amen.

2. To become more righteous, work on becoming more God-conscious:
   - First, memorize and remind yourself daily of Isaiah 41:10: *"Don't be afraid, for **I am with you**. Don't be discouraged, for I am your God. I will strengthen you and help you. I will hold you up with my victorious right hand"* (NLT).

   - Also, follow the example of Brother Lawrence, the writer of *The Practice of the Presence of God*. Throughout the day, engage in a continual, friendly conversation with your Father; endeavoring to do nothing, say nothing, and think nothing that is displeasing to Him.

3. Memorize Job's pronouncement and declare it over yourself every day:
   "I will maintain my righteousness and never let go of it; my conscience will not reproach me as long as I live" (Job 27:6 NIV).

4. Ask the Lord to show you the 'issues' at the root of your struggle to be a person of godly character.

5. Daily declare your intentions to be a person of honor and integrity by announcing:
   I am a person of character; I fight battles small and large and win. I was chosen by God to be a conqueror, and He has equipped me to for the task. I may not feel like a winner, but I am. I may not look like a champion, but, nevertheless, I am. It does not matter whether others think of me as a winner; I am one! I will accomplish my task ... I will complete my mission ... and I will finish strong for I am God's knight in shining honor!

In the next chapter ...
You will discover the incredible future that God has prepared for you and find out why *extreme success* is your birthright and how to get on track for success regardless of your present position.

Chapter 7
Extreme Success — Your Birthright

Success is God's plan for your life based on the destiny He created especially for you. You might remember His promise in Jeremiah 29:11: *I will bless you with a future filled with hope — a future of success, not of suffering* (CEV). Jesus described God's intentions toward you in John 10:10, when he said: *"The thief does not come except to steal, and to kill, and to destroy. I have come that they may have life, and that they may have it more abundantly"* (NKJV).

Bible teacher and Greek scholar, Rick Renner expands the meaning of "life abundantly" with the following amplification:

> … I came that they might have, keep, and constantly retain a vitality, gusto, vigor and zest for living that springs up from deep down inside. I came that they might embrace this unrivaled, unequaled, matchless, incomparable, richly loaded and overflowing life to the ultimate maximum.

Can there be any doubt? God intends for you to live a *maximized* life of 'extreme success!' But, what is success *really*?

Our culture has defined success to mean accumulating wealth, acquiring power, and obtaining the trappings of the "rich and famous." In other words, success is all about *our personal gratification*. The Lord, however, has a more profound and deeply satisfying definition. His description of success often contains wealth, power, and nice stuff, but it goes beyond those superficial things to include that which brings ultimate satisfaction, deep fulfillment, and lasting joy. We call it, "Extreme Success!"

The cultural meaning of success falls short of God's because it does not take into consideration a person's accountability for their life's relationships — with God, spouse, and offspring. In fact, regardless of how good people are at acquiring wealth, power, and 'toys,' if they fail in *any* of their primary relationships, they are actually a complete failure in life. A key to Extreme Success is getting your priorities right or, to use a phrase found in the Scriptures, it's about putting your affections in order:
> Set your affection on things above, not on things on the earth
> (Colossians 3:2 KJV).

Jesus clarified our priorities in Matthew 22:37-39, with this requirement:
> ... You shall love the Lord your God with all your heart, and with all your soul, and with all your mind. This is the great and foremost commandment. The second is like it, you shall love your neighbor as yourself (NASB).

When loving God becomes your first priority, other things in your life will naturally fall into their proper place.

WOMEN ONLY
Just as success in life looks different for variously talented men, it can have a variety of meanings for women. The model of a godly woman found in Proverbs 31, although written many millennia ago, is still God's idea of a successful woman. You will notice that she is not chained to the home whose only duty is to care for her husband and children. In fact, the Proverbs 31 woman was many things ...
Importer ▫ Supervisor ▫ Real estate investor ▫ Creative designer
Manufacture ▫ Salesperson ▫ Benefactor to the poor ▫ And more
Extreme Success, for both men and women, has the same

component ... the right priorities in their relationships: God first, family second, careers third. The right balance causes your pursuit of success to fall into its proper place. Many women have believed they must sacrifice their dreams and goals, or put them on the back burner, if they marry and have a family, but that is not what the Bible teaches.

However, many men and women in our 'self-first' society have gone to the opposite extreme and placed their desires above their primary relationships. This has caused shipwrecked lives and broken families which should come as no surprise because the Bible warns, "For what does it profit a man [or woman] to gain the whole world, and forfeit his soul? (Mark 8:36 NASB).

There is no real success apart from God and His purposes for your life. You have to be more than a token Christian to enjoy extreme success; you have to be sold out to His will for your life and your destiny. You must put the spiritual first and the material second, or you to can become another person with trapping of success but only a vague relationship with God.

Risky Business

Pursuing success is the greatest challenge that many men face. God intended for men to be risk-takers and to teach their sons and daughters to take *acceptable* risks. In fact, He demands that each person risk everything on faith in His goodness and good intentions toward them:

> *For I know the plans I have for you, declares the LORD, plans for welfare and not for evil, to give you a future and a hope* (Jeremiah 29:11 ESV).

One of the greatest examples of a risk-taker who put his trust in God and achieved extreme success is David. He walked on a battlefield without a *real* weapon, a shield, or body armor to face the deadliest warrior in either army. However, David's faith in God was so extreme that he *ran* to meet Goliath clasping only a shepherd boy's weapon — his slingshot.

You might dismiss David's super-human courage as reasonable in light of his anointing to be king. However, we also have a king's anointing according to Revelation 1:6. You may think that you could never be a great champion, but the same God who formed David into a champion and equipped him for success wants to prepare you for *extreme success*, too. The issue is never how big (think of little Dave vs. the giant) or how experienced or even how well-educated *you* are, but how big *your God is*.

Most of us consider relying on God's power only after we have used up all of our own strength; at the end of our rope, we call upon Him. However, if God is *first* in your life, you should call upon Him *first*, knowing that He will show up and do what He does best — either provide a miracle deliverance, or walk with you through the crisis to an 'expected end'! God does not want us to look at *our* strength and *our* abilities as the deciding factor in whether we should pursue the dreams He gives us, but rather to focus on *His* leading, *His* strength, and *His* abilities.

Do not fall for the lie that poverty and a humble status in life are necessary to spirituality. David became a man of great power, position, and incredible wealth. He went from the keeper of his father's sheep to the divinely appointed shepherd of God's Chosen People. And, the Lord has appointed a great future for you, too!

Although it is unlikely that you will become a king and amass the wealth that David had, you too will have the opportunity to succeed in life. Scripture indicates that God gives every person an opportunity to …
>Reach his full potential in a career path
>Be successful as a husband
>Raise kids who 'hit the mark'
>Build a family business
>Become an influencer of men and women.
>Build Christian relationships
>Becoming engaged in some form of ministry

One of my (Bart's) favorite examples of success is Tim Tebow, the national championship-winning quarter back of the University of Florida. In addition to his talents in football, Tim is a committed Christian whose parents are missionaries and whose brother works with Campus Crusade for Christ.

Tim even writes Scripture verses on his face during games to help keep himself focused on eternal values. He is a great example of how a person can represent their faith without being 'preachy' or overbearing while operating in the glare of publicity.

WOMEN ONLY

In past chapters, we mentioned that women are, for the most part, risk-adverse. Perhaps, God created women in that way to provide balance for their risk-taking husbands. A wise man consults with his wife before taking risks and then, based on his beliefs and her comments, pursues what he believes to be the best course of action for his family (first) and himself.

Women with careers can profit from consulting with their husbands or fathers about taking risks. When God joins a man and woman together, a synergism occurs that makes them wiser and better as a team than they could possibly be as individuals.

Taking risks is a natural part of life. However, the risks a gambler takes with only the slim hope of getting lucky (whether at the gaming tables, with investments, or in business) is a foolish risk.

How Do You Spell Success?

Worldly success, as we mentioned before, is defined as position, power, and wealth. Success is NOT the size of your ambitions. Success in life is much, much more ...

Success is being and doing what God planned for you; submitting to His will for your life and destiny; hearing God and obeying what He says.

Our real success will be measured when we stand before our Heavenly Father for judgment, and He either says:

"Well done good and faithful servant!" or

"You made it to Heaven but did not carryout your purpose on earth."

Consider for a moment the significance of that coming event and, if you need to, repent of living primarily for yourself. Make a solemn vow before God that you will turn from your old selfish ways and begin to live your life the way He intended.

God spelled out His definition of success in Jeremiah 9:23,24 when He explained:

> ... *Don't let the wise boast in their wisdom, or the powerful boast in their power, or the rich boast in their riches. But let him who glories **glory in this: that he understands and knows Me** [personally and practically, directly discerning and recognizing My character], that I am the Lord, Who practices loving-kindness, judgment, and righteousness in the earth, for in these things I delight, says the Lord.* (AMP, emphasis added).

Get it? Success is personally *knowing* God. Obviously, this "knowing" goes well beyond salvation, as important as that is. His view of success is completely different from ours. In fact, it is so different that we can have difficulty making sense of it and wonder what "knowing God" has to do with the success of people who are *not* 'called' to full-time ministry. "Knowing God," however, goes well beyond a clerical vocation. It is about being in a *trusting* relationship with Him.

Why is 'trust' important to God? The Creator could give Himself anything; however, what He wants most is something that cannot be obtained by exercising His creative power — ***God wants friends who will partner with Him in His purpose for the earth.***

God wants the kind of friends who won't let Him down, who won't turn their backs on Him, and who are not in the relationship for what they can get out of it. Simply put, He wants the same kind of friend that you want: a person who loves Him for who He is, not what He can give. A friend like Solomon who, when given the chance to get anything he wanted, asked for character and the wisdom to fulfill his calling. And because Solomon was a *real* friend, God also gave him wealth and favor beyond imagination. How did God know that He could trust Solomon with riches? A *real friend* of God knows that all earthly riches are nothing compared to the value of friendship with the Lord.

WOMEN ONLY
Women, for the most part, have greater intuition than men do. Consequently, they are more in tune with the spirit world and have a greater natural sensitivity to God than men. This means women often hear His voice quicker than men can, and are more intuitive about spiritual things than the majority men.

What's Love Got To Do With It?
God's desire for relationship goes deeper than our understanding of friendship and is actually more like the intimate connection between lovers. The scripture (Jeremiah 9:23,24) which declares real success is "knowing God," means exactly what it says. The Amplified Bible gives us more insight when it elaborates on the word translated "knowing" by adding the phrase: *"personally and practically, directly discerning and recognizing my character."* From this definition, we can see that "knowing" God goes beyond an intellectual understanding of Him and actually refers to "knowing" in the more intimate sense.

Yada, the Hebrew word used in this scripture for "knowing," is the same word used in Genesis 4:1 where it says, *"... Adam knew* [yada] *Eve his wife, and she conceived and bore Cain ...."* To get a richer understanding, remove the thought of sex from *yada* and replace it with the idea of an *intimate union.*

Consider that *real* intimacy is about love and that sex, at its best, is merely an expression of the love and intimacy experienced between a husband and wife. Perhaps you can remember when you first realized that you loved the person who became your mate. When you thought of him or her, you may have unconsciously smiled and experienced a warm feeling. We can have, and need to have, this same kind of intimacy with God.

Now we have the tools to begin to understand the Lord's definition of success: a relationship so *intimate* and tender that, when you turn your thoughts to Him, you *feel* love. In addition, you know and appreciate God's love for you.

His love is so deep that He gave the thing most precious to Him (His Son) to save you from the judgment you deserve for your sins. However, He went beyond merely providing salvation from a sinner's hell ... God adopted you into His family as a beloved son or daughter.

Are you thinking, "That sounds too good to be true" and wondering if there's a catch? Oh, yes. There certainly *is* a catch. You see, your God is jealous of your love, adoration, and worship and He refuses to take second place to any other person or thing. In Exodus 20:15, He warns, *"... You shall worship no other God, for the LORD, whose name is Jealous, is a jealous God ..."* (ESV).

What kinds of things might He be jealous of in *your* life? We can make gods of *people*, *possessions*, and even *desires*. Yes, God expects you to love your wife, but not more than you love Him. (That was Adam's sin.) The Bible says that the snake did not deceive Adam but when Adam saw that Eve had sinned, he loved her so much that he chose separation from God over separation from her. (Yes, we can love people too much when we place them ahead of God.)

Which of your *possessions* would you have to think twice about giving away should the Lord ask it of you — your car, your home, your phone, your savings? Yes, God requires you to put Him above, not only the things you enjoy, but even those things you feel you 'must' have and cannot live without.

God cannot be your *EVERYTHING*
if you withhold *ANYTHING* from Him.

Look at the *desires* of your heart; they may be sinful lusts or legitimate wishes. Obviously, you have to say an emphatic, "NO!" to your lusts but even your most legitimate desires cannot be allowed to be more important than the Lord.

What has driven you to become the person you are today? Think about it. God will not take second place to your desires *or the pursuit of your unfulfilled needs*. However, when you place Him above the desires of your heart, God promises:

> *Delight yourself in the LORD; And He will give you the desires of your heart* (Psalms 37:4 NASB).

Not many people pursue the *Extreme Success* that comes through knowing God this way, and so they fail to enjoy the benefits this 'knowing' creates ... but how about you?

WOMEN ONLY
Perhaps the feminine desire for intimacy rather than its masculine counterpart, the drive for sex, makes it easier for women to be close to God. This could be a reason that women seem more spiritually inclined than men. If you have not yet discovered intimacy with God, seek him as ardently as you would a lover, and He will come as close as you allow.

Do not fall into the trap of thinking that God will pursue you for intimacy as a man might. Oh, yes, He will seek you for salvation but, after that, you must be the aggressor and go after Him with all your heart to develop a relationship of intimacy.

How Are You *Spending* Your Life?
While it is true that 'money is power' there is a far more important and arresting truth — *TIME IS LIFE.* You have been allotted a limited number of years to accomplish your God-given purposes on this earth, and you are trading your *life* for the things to you give your *time* to. Are you making a wise trade? Stop and consider for a moment how you spend each of your precious days and nights. Are you living as if every minute is valuable and every hour priceless?

When you add 8 hours for sleep to 8 hours for employment then subtract it from 24 hours that leaves you about 8 hours per day or 56 hours a week (including weekends) to spend on other things. So, what are you doing during your waking hours away from work? Do you spend them ...

> at work (anyway)?
> at play (with your friends)?
> at home (in front of the TV)?

with your children?
with your spouse?
at church or in ministry activities?

Are you trading your life for *extreme success* or merely for momentary pleasure? Are you giving your time and efforts to fulfill your responsibility to be a good husband and father and the things God is asking of you, or spending your time pleasing yourself? Are you accomplishing what He has for you to do in this season of your life? If you hesitate to answer and cannot say a confident "Yes," then the answer is probably "No." But, it is never too late to repent and turn your life around. God has even promised to "redeem" time for those who love Him.

Dancing on the Sword of Success
Success can be like a razor-sharp, two-edged sword. If you mishandle success, it can cut you open before you even feel the pain or recognize that you are wounded. A person's greatest tests often come during times of promotion and success. Most people do not fail during the tough times, because difficulties call forth the best in a person. In fact, the one who fails during bad times is often self-destructive and/or running away from their issues.

Men (and some women) typically set their priorities for success in this order — job, finances, and family. However, to escape a painful slash from the sword of success, we have to reverse the order:
1. Family
2. Finances
3. Job

This new priority gives first place to the things God considers most important and it encourages us to make the best use of our time from His vantage point. Most men are willing to make the effort necessary for success, but many are confused about how to best allocate their time and energies. If asked why they are working 12-hour days, they might tell you they are doing it to achieve financial independence so they can have more time to spend with their families. However, their goal is within their reach right now, if they would only reverse the order of their priorities.

Most men (and some women) do not feel validated unless they achieve success. Each person develops a unique, individual definition of success that is based on his/her life perspective. For some, it means having a great home in the right neighborhood, others think about expensive cars and boats. Some people consider exciting vacations or exotic cruises a sign of success; yet others link it to prestige and impressing the 'right' people with their significance.

Think about it, then answer the following question before reading on — What do you *honestly* consider the marks of success (without getting religious about it)?

What is it you 'gotta have' to consider yourself a success? Now take that 'gotta-have' compulsion and re-formulate it based on the priorities that produce *Extreme Success*, and you will be a *real* winner!

As a minister for going on 50 years, I (Henry) have stood by the bedside of many dying people. I have heard some cry out with guilt and pain because they did not spend their lives on those things that create *real* success. But, I have never heard anyone say, "Bring my check book to me, and tell me how much money I have," or "Tell me all the great things I accomplished in life." But I have heard many say, "Oh, I wish to God that I had spent more time with my spouse and children." It was too late for them, but *you* ... you still have time to correct mistaken priorities.

WOMEN ONLY
Some women have bought into the feminist notion of success and believe they 'must have' a successful career outside the home to be validated as a person of worth. Although this may be true for some, it is certainly not true for all. Some are called to be full-time nurturers to their children and helpmates to their husbands. A woman must find out what God has planned for her and set her goals accordingly.

The Sacrifices of Success

When a man pursues God's Extreme Success, his marriage, children, and spiritual life will never suffer. However, those who put their job's first will make sacrifices they never intended in order to achieve goals that never truly satisfy. Their drive for success will, at some point, require them to throw aside their integrity, 'walk over' their associates, sacrifice their relationships with their wives, and fail as fathers.

When such a man finally reaches the summit of 'success,' he will make a disappointing discovery — it was a mirage. When he reaches for the satisfaction for which he worked so hard and gave up so much, his hands close on emptiness. He cannot even feel pride in his accomplishments or enjoy his level of success, because all he can see is the people above him, who have achieved more. While chasing the phantom of so-called success, however, he will have become a stranger to his wife and children.

I (Bart), early on, had a mentor who one day told me that he could walk into any store and buy anything he wanted. Although my *ultimate* goal was to achieve financial independence by age 35 with be ability to retire (should I want to), the capacity to walk into *any* store and buy *anything* became my *intermediate* goal.

One day after turning 30 years old, I walked into a very exclusive store in the upscale Galleria Mall in Dallas and looked around and smiled because I knew I had attained that 'goal.' I could buy anything there I wanted. However, I discovered that, when I actually bought things in those exclusive stores, it didn't feel any different from buying from a discount store. I got more of a thrill out of carrying the bag with their logo on it down the street, than I did from what was inside the bag. The thing I believed would bring me so much satisfaction turned out to be meaningless.

Even though I was scrupulously ethical in my pursuit of wealth, and gave much of the money I earned to ministries, I was a failure from God's standpoint because I had put my success ahead of my relationship with Him. He gave me 10 years of grace before He knocking over my 'house of cards'; then I then submitted to His will and entered full-time ministry.

Two Little-recognized Secrets for Godly Success:

First — Eliminate Pride and Cultivate Humility

There was no way that I (Bart) could have remained in the business world and cultivated humility.

- Pride brags: "By my skills, my strength, and savvy, I will achieve success."
- Ego boasts: "Everything in the world worth noticing is about me."
- The world insists: "Success is about self-promotion and self-gratification."

The four-letter word for success in our culture is S-E-L-F. However, God's four-letter word for success is L-I-F-E. James, the brother of Jesus, explained how important humility is to Extreme Success when he penned: *"… God opposes the proud, but gives grace to the humble"* (James 4:6 ESV). *Grace* means "heaven's supernatural help." God promises you help beyond the natural when you are humble.

It is *not* wrong to want to achieve, or have a burning passion to accomplish and build, as long as it is not more important than your relationship with God. He wants us to use our passions as He directs. What we are capable of accomplishing on our own is minor compared to what we can do when co-laboring with Him, doing *His* thing … *His* way … with *His* help.

Pride is a fracture in the soul through which the enemy can wiggle. Even the thing you feel you could never be tempted with, can be twisted into a soul gap created by pride. Some men who, in their wildest imaginations, would never consider a homosexual relationship have discovered that pride can be manipulated to even make room for a male lover.

Second — Learn What to do When God Says, "No"

King David had a desire to build a resting place for the Ark of the Covenant, a temple to God … but God said, "No." Although God had very likely placed that desire in David's heart, Scripture tells us that the Lord denied him that privilege because, he was a "man of war" (seen 1 Chronicles 28:3) and had "shed blood." Possibly God was referring in part to him causing the death of Bathsheba's husband, Uriah's.

What we do know is that David became a "man of war" at God's direction and had "shed blood" while defeating Israel's enemies. So, it would have been easy for Him to take offense at the Lord's rejection. He could have complained, "After all the hardships I've been through for You; the times I've put my life on the line to do Your will, and You won't allow me build You a temple *at my own expense!*" He could have become offended at God and ... but he didn't.

Consider the case of Moses: He tried to do the right thing by defending a fellow Israelite and ended up killing an Egyptian, then had to flee. Although trained to be a ruler and called to be Israel's savior, he spent decades tending another man's sheep on the backside of the desert. After the "burning bush" experience, Moses faced down the most powerful man in the Middle East (Pharaoh) ... led Israel out of Egypt ... put up with their complaining for 40 years ... and saved them many times from extermination by God's wrath. Yet when he made one seemingly insignificant mistake, God denied him the privilege of completing his assignment of taking Israel into the Promised Land. Moses could have easily been offended with God but he wasn't.

What will *you* do when God says, "No" to ...
- The promotion you deserve?
- A much-needed financial breakthrough?
- The healing of a dying loved one?
- Saving your marriage?
- Changing your spouse?
- Fixing your kids?

Nothing is too hard for God. He can easily give you what you want and need. So what will your response be when God 'disappoints' *you*? Or, instead of talking about a future event, perhaps, we should ask how you have reacted when God denied your sincere request for His help in the past.

If this were merely a scholastic exercise, I'm sure you could write the correct answer but this question is not academic — it's authentic. This is *real* life! And, if you get this answer wrong, it will derail you from the successes God has scheduled for your future and could even cost you your life.

YES, LIFE IS A TEST!

So, how will you respond when God disappoints you? Will you blame Him, yourself, or the devil and say …

- I just didn't pray hard enough
- I didn't ask often enough
- The enemy is holding back my answer
- Blah, Blah, Blah ….

Most of the time, when God says, "No" to our reasonable request, it is not a brick wall with a Dead End sign painted on it, but rather an invitation to turn the corner and go in a new direction.

At times, God's, "No" merely means "not now." When our prayer request involves others, it could be that someone else is saying, "No" (God never forces people to do anything against their will.) Sometimes we get a "no" because our request is not His will, and sometimes our motives are wrong:

> "You ask and do not receive, because you ask with wrong motives, so that you may spend it on your pleasures" (James 4:3 NASB).

Regardless of the reason for God's "No" — *it is a test*. And the important question is not "Why" but "Will"? Will you become offended? Or, will you be like Moses and accept His decision whether you understand the reason for it or not? Will you be like David, embrace God's "No," and be satisfied accumulating the materials for a temple that another person will build?

**Your response to God's "No" will determine
if He can later trust you with His "Yes."**

You should probably read the foregoing sentence again and again until it really sinks in, because only those with a *pure heart* toward God are candidates for His extravagant blessings — you cannot *afford* (in every sense of that word) to be mad at Him.

It is easy to become offended for a family member or other people. Let me (Bart) tell you the story of a young woman I'll call "Jet." She grew up in church, and her parents were good Christian people. In fact, her mother served in both the children and youth ministries, and her father volunteered as well. However, Jet saw a lot of hypocrisy in the church, and a time came when some Christian leaders treated her parents and others badly.

She became angry with them and eventually even became angry with God. She figured that, since He was ultimately in control and saw what happened to her parents and did nothing to protect them; He must not be "good" as she had been taught. By the time Jet was 20, she had completely rebelled against the church and her parents, and was living an immoral lifestyle. She was using alcohol, drugs, and sex to escape what she termed, "those people's rules." Jet's parents worked through their personal hurts and were able to move on but, the last I heard, Jet was still stuck in her anger with God and man. Do you have anything in common with Jet?

Tips for Extreme Success
- Success is good when it is a promotion from God, but bad when it is something we achieved through compromising our integrity.
- Success can never be our primary motivation but must be seen as a means to accomplish God's work and care for others.
- The wrong kind of success will give us a false sense of self-sufficiency rooted in pride.
- Success, whether the good or bad kind, will bring with it our greatest opportunity to sin.
- Everyone makes small or large mistakes occasionally but the way you deal with your mistakes reveals the kind of person you are and your future success.

- If promotion or success makes you a leader, then you are responsible for any harm your mistakes have on other people.
- Pursuing success is a good thing when the pursuit of God has first place in your life.

True success is leaving a legacy that lives on after you. Will others remember you, and what you have accomplished, after your death? I want my life to affect many for good and for God ... how about you?

Action Steps

1. Take a minute to clear your mind and pray this prayer from your heart:
   Jesus, I ask you to open my mind to understand Your definition of Extreme Success. In my heart, I truly desire to be a person of significance, but without the right priorities, I know that I will hurt others and myself. So, I ask for Your help. To the best of my ability, I give You my future. I give You the freedom to adjust my perspective and direction. Help me to find the extreme success that You have planned for my life. Amen.

2. Early in the chapter, I asked you to think about your definition of success. Write out the definition of success by which you have lived up until now. Then, beneath it, create a revised definition that takes into account what you have learned in this chapter.

3. Write down the motivational factors that drive your desire for success. Ask God to show you hidden underlying wants or needs that you are trying to meet through success.

4. Since life = time, write the answer to the question: How are you spending your life? Actually, calculate how you have been spending your free time (about 56 hours), using the last seven days as a model. Beneath that, note how you would like to begin making a better use of your free time and create a detailed plan for how you will carry out those changes.

5. If you feel that something is standing between you and intimacy with God, ask Him to reveal what is barring you from the closeness you desire. The cause could be any number of things, but be open to the possibility that you have a buried offense, secret sin, or an area of life that you need to surrender to Him.

In the final chapter …
You will discover the HIGH way to Manhood when you learn about the "Rite of Passage" and find out why it is of great value and not an antiquated way of looking at maturity. If you have never experienced this initiation or confirmation of manhood, you will be happy to hear that, regardless of your age, it is never too late. Mothers can also learn the important role they play at this crucial time in their son's life.

Chapter 8
The HIGHway to Manhood

Our society makes little of the transition from boyhood to manhood. It is often lumped into what we think of as the 'teen' years. However, this transition is best made through a tangible 'Rite of Passage.' The culture-wide nonexistence of this practice creates uncertainty among young men about how to cross over into manhood, and it even causes adult men to wonder if they have completed the transition. Understanding the Rite of Passage is important not only to men but also to mothers and wives, because they have a supportive role essential to the process. Rite of Passage is not merely a ceremony but a journey that leads a boy into manhood.

Maturing or Manhood, What's the Difference?

Most men, if pressed to explain when that happened, cannot name a time or place and might say something like: "I just wandered into it. I woke up one day, and I was (20, 30, 40) years old and figured that I must be a man." However, you can never just 'wander into' manhood or arrive there by accident, because this road is a narrow way which is easily missed. Consequently, many men feel uneasy about their masculinity; some suffer from gender confusion; and others have mistakenly defined manhood as "macho."

I (Henry) have worked with men in their forties (and older) who were still little boys in their actions and thoughts. Many of these men remained emotionally tied to their mothers. One man I ministered to went to his mother's house after work each day for dinner before going home to his wife. He excused it by saying that his wife was a bad cook. After ministry, he was eventually able to let go of his mother and *"...cleave to his wife..."* as Genesis 2:24, says a man should do.

Because our culture often mistakes *physical maturity* for manhood, we sometimes attribute the Rite of Passage to first-time events in the adult world, such as:

- Getting a driver's license
- Beginning to date
- Losing virginity
- Finishing school
- Getting a job
- Joining the Army

But none of these things is capable of creating a defining moment of transition to manhood. *While maturing is vital to a man, it is not the same as manhood.*

Perhaps you have seen on television or in *National Geographic,* the rituals used by ancient cultures for creating the transition to manhood. During these Rites of Passage, African tribes and other native peoples mark their bodies, send their boys out to hunt (and live) or live in the wilds with only minimal equipment, or require the completion of other tests that indicate a boy's readiness to join the 'company of men.' Although these rituals may seem unsophisticated, and even unnecessary to modern thought, nevertheless, they are effective in creating that 'moment of transition' between childhood and adulthood.

Knowing the moment of transition is important to young men. The most basic element of graduation into manhood is the understanding that a boy has met the standard of his culture to be considered a man. Only men who have already made the transition are qualified to call a boy to be a man; just being male is not enough. To be effective, it should include an understanding of male history:

- An appreciation of the accomplishment of your forefathers.
- An understanding of what the Lord requires of a man.

A Rite of Passage must call the *male spirit* within a boy to assert itself. This requires a boy to leave the company of women and children, and be joined to (and identify with) the brotherhood of men. The Apostle Paul, speaking of that transition in 1 Corinthians 13:11, explained: *"When I was a child, I used to speak like a child, think like a child, reason like a child; when I became a man, I did away with childish things"* (NASB). Boys, who would be men, must put away irresponsibility, self-indulgence, and childish thinking and acting.

WOMEN ONLY

Because mother is often the primary caregiver, boys often spend more time with their mothers than their fathers. Consequently, they form a dependent relationship with "Mom." That is normal but, during the passage into manhood, dependence needs to be detached from the mother and redirected to the father (or a father figure).

This does not mean that the boy will stop loving and respecting his mother, but that he will begin the process of learning to relate to her in a way appropriate for an independent man, not a dependent boy. This is imperative for a healthy relationship between a mother and her adult son. If a boy must stumble along the road to manhood on his own, without the aid of a knowledgeable mother and father (or father figure) this can be a very painful time for both mother and son.

The traditional Jewish culture provides us a model: soon after Bar Mitzvah (when the boy turns 12), the father takes over rearing the boy. This redirects the nurturing bond with the mother to a masculine bond with the father who becomes his teacher and mentor. Because this is not practiced in our culture, a boy can spend long years, and go to great extremes to break free from his mother. Those who never achieve this goal may struggle with gender confusion and other dysfunctional behavior.

Most mothers find it difficult not to comfort a son struggling to find manhood. However, it is vitally important that she not undermine this process with well meaning emotional support that encourages her son to remain attached to her rather than become a man.

One African tribe conducts the Rite of Passage in this way: when a boy is about 13-years-old, the men of the tribe dress up in masks and go to the mother's hut and call him outside. Should he fail to come out on his own, they forcibly remove him from his mother. The men take all the boys far into the jungle for three months where they teach them hunting, fishing, and farming by day and the tribal legends at night. This is how the young men learn the stories of their fathers. Before they are allowed to return to the village, each boy is required to recite the tribal legends. The Rite of Passage is then completed upon the selection of a wife. The father helps his son, the newly-made man, to build separates huts for himself and his wife. Although they each can enter the other's hut, they sleep in their own place. When children are born, they must sleep with their mother, and so the cycle continues, generation to generation.

A Code of Honor
Manhood is about *responsibility.* Real men live by a code of honor that encompasses both God-given and natural responsibilities. For example: no one has to check on the way I (Bart) relate to my wife and children to make certain that I am doing the right things. Nor does anyone have to check the websites I visit, the places I go to, or what I watch on television, because I live by a code of honor. The Lord, and those to whom I am accountable have defined my honor code, and it is inscribed on my heart. Manhood requires men to live by a code of ethical conduct.

The Scripture says that people of the New Covenant no longer live by external rules but by the rules God has written upon our hearts. In other words, a man's honor code comes from an *internal compass,* or conscience, that governs him from within. It directs thoughts, attitudes, and actions and gives us the desire to uphold a standard of integrity.

This honor code, however, does not come out of fear of disapproval and/or discipline, but rather from an internal desire to make ourselves pleasing to God. Although such a desire may be a new idea to some, the attainment of true manhood requires this quality.

Children, and immature adults, must have rules and regulations enforced *externally* because their *internal compass* is undeveloped. The one who attains *real* manhood, however, has learned to do what is right despite personal desires or outside influences. Thus, integrity of character is a defining point of manhood. The spirit of manhood comes from the Spirit of our Father God. Acts 10:38, describes Jesus (the model for manhood) as a person who, " *... went around doing good ...*" (NIV), and *real* men do the same thing.

WOMEN ONLY
When God made Adam and Eve, He gave to humanity both male and female aspects of Himself. He intends for fathers and mothers to be a complete expression of God to their children. Some feminists believe that a father is unnecessary for child-rearing. However, even a supermom cannot replace a father in a boy's or girl's life. The Lord believes so strongly in the family unit that He promised, in Psalms 68:5,6, to be a: "Father to the fatherless, ..." and to place "... the lonely in families; ..." (NLT).
Based on this scripture and others, we know God wants every child to have the influence of a godly father and should the biological father be missing, we believe that He will provide a father-figure.

A father and a mother each make a unique contribution to their children. Fathers primarily bestow worth on their children and if they fail to give it, their sons and daughters will look for it in 'all the wrong places.' Their quest is doomed to failure, however, until they find their Heavenly Father. Only He can supply what the natural father did not provide, and much more.

I (Henry) once ministered to a woman whose father never gave her his approval. He was always critical and impossible to please. When she began to mature, he refused to hug or hold her. Her mother tried to compensate for the lack of fatherly love but, predictably, it did not help. In her teens, she became very spiteful and later had a child out-of-wedlock. All this could probably been avoided had her father given her the love, acceptance, and approval she so desperately needed.

The "D" Word — Discipline

Manhood requires *self*-government. Those raised in permissive homes often find it difficult to learn self-discipline. The importance of discipline has, for the most part, been misunderstood in our culture. Some so-called 'experts' have discouraged the use of discipline, saying that it stifles creativity and freedom of expression. Yet, those raised without discipline often fail to appreciate their gifts and abilities, and they rarely have the stamina essential to create or accomplishing anything of value.

From age 16 to 26, I (Bart) had an excess of ambition; the 'need to succeed' drove most of my actions. Winning, being first in everything (sports or business) consumed me. Consequently, anyone who tried to block me either got out-of-the-way or wished they had. I was so *overly* competitive that, for example, no one wanted to play board games with me. I was determined to achieve my goals. As we say in Texas, "I was gonna win, come hell or high water"! My desire to succeed was obsessive and drove me to excel. Lack of success in any area represented to me the failure to be a man, and endangered the validation I so desperately wanted.

(Henry's comments) This compulsion to succeed almost destroyed Bart's life — his relationships with God, family, and friends. Personal achievements or success does not make a man; manhood comes from the heart — not from what our hands accomplish.

I (Bart) mentioned in a previous chapter how the Lord eventually redirected my manhood to Himself, and imparted to me the Spirit of Adoption. From this experience I finally learned that my manhood is not based on what I do, but on who I am — God's son, created in His image for His purpose.

Jacob, the son of Isaac and brother of Esau, had a similar problem. He was willing to do almost anything to get the Birthright and Blessing of his father — he deceived, lied, cheated, and stole. Jacob's *moral compass* was twisted around his insecurities and desires. Insecurities and desires are the primary things that skew every man's internal compass. Just as God worked in Jacob's heart during the decades he served his abusive father-in-law, God is working in each of us to write *His* precepts upon our hearts.

WOMEN ONLY

Mothers are often on the frontlines of administering discipline. So Mom (and Dad), don't be afraid to hold your young son (ages three to five) accountable for his actions. Learning to accept responsibility is vital to achieving the self-government required for manhood. If your son does not receive such correction then, as a teenager, he could break your heart.

Single mothers who feel sorry for their fatherless sons, or feel guilty for working, can have a difficult time getting their sons to follow the rules. However, you must give him the gift of discipline; it is the truest expression of love you can make.

If you are a single mom, get help:
Read Christian books about discipline
Seek advice from a those who have more maturity in this area (perhaps your parents)
Consult with your pastor or a trusted friend.
Regardless of what it may take, it is imperative that you find the courage to discipline!

If your husband has abdicated his responsibilities in this area, then address the issue with him and try to develop a plan to stop permissive and/or rebellious behavior. It is doubly hard (and sometimes impossible) to turn the tide of rebellion in a teenage boy struggling to become a man.

Simple, direct, and immediate consequences for a child's actions are the best approach to punishment. In addition, both fathers and mothers must be consistent with their discipline or their correction will cause confusion. Because the human heart has not changed since Adam's expulsion from The Garden, Solomon's advice on child-rearing remains valid: "Discipline your children while you still have the chance; indulging them destroys them" (Proverbs 19:18 MSG).

Discipline is so important that mothers and fathers cannot allow their desire for their children's love to rob them of the will to discipline.

Defining Manhood

Manhood means becoming a person who is centered and capable of ...

- Relating to the society of men
- Assuming responsibilities
- Having a healthy relationship with women
- Establishing a mature relationship with the Lord
- Taking his place in the local church and Body of Christ
- Pursuing the work for which God has gifted him
- Engaging in fatherhood and leadership of the home

Manhood is a journey, and every man should continue working to become more of a man, more: balanced, committed, dedicated, fruitful, secure, principled, loving, trusting, trustworthy, honest, genuine, and disciplined.

Freedom From the Feminine Force

The lack of understanding in our culture about a young man's need to break free from dependence on the feminine influence, and to bond with the masculine, has produced disastrous results. Men, who fail to learn how to relate to a woman properly, will never fully find their manhood

Although embracing the masculine can be a difficult balance for a young man, the man who fails to break free from the feminine spirit will be constantly looking for masculine affirmation *from women* and that is something a woman can never give. Such men become prime candidates for sexual addictions.

Getting affirmation through sexuality is the quickest way for a boy to *seem* to verify his manhood but, in reality, it is the worst thing that could happen. Men who become slaves to *sexual affirmation* are mastered by a feminine spirit, and they are easily persuaded to follow any demands because of their 'weak hearts.' Being addicted to 'womb comfort' will always make such a man dependent upon a woman, and never allow him to assume his rightful place as her leader and protector.

Breaking free from the feminine spirit is only half of this challenge; the other half is bonding with the masculine spirit. Some men have confused male bonding with a sexual relationship, and misunderstood the role men should play in their lives. Those who have over-bonded with their mothers and found *emotional* intimacy with them may seek unnatural intimacy in their relationships with men. This is at the root of some men's susceptibility to homosexuality. Dysfunctional attempts to becoming a man, invariably lead to twisted definitions of manhood.

I (Henry) once ministered to a 40-year-old man raised in a home with a controlling and domineering mother and a weak father. The mother refused to allow the father to teach his son how to play sports, because she was overly concerned that he might get hurt. The father eventually gave up trying to be head of the family. Without a strong masculine model to follow, the boy fell into a confused state of manhood and became homosexual. As far as I know, he has never broken free from that lifestyle.

Men who find themselves described in this section do not have to continue in homosexuality or sexual addiction, you can be free! Freedom is found by first understanding how and why you came to the place you are at. (Ask God to reveal it to you) The second step is to deal with the core issues at the base of your lifestyle and to find fulfillment of from your Heaven Father. There are many organizations that can be helpful and some churches have ministries of this kind. Exodusinternational.org is a website that helps connect people with those who can help.

WOMEN ONLY

The difficult truth for some mothers is: every son must break away from the feminine influence of his mother to become a man. Although letting go is difficult, it is the only way to insure that he will someday return to you as a man who loves and respects his mother.

Fear makes letting go very difficult, and experiences of loss and betrayal by men can contribute to that fear. However, the more one holds on, the more the boy will 'act out' to be free. Boys know instinctually that they must become independent of their mothers in order to become men. The more difficult this is, the more damaging it will be to a future relationship with her son.

Any woman reading this book who has suffered a difficult break with her son can take comfort in the fact that Jesus can restore any broken relationship. If you are ready to repent and ask His healing spirit to enter those wounded places in your life, you might want to pray this prayer:

Lord Jesus, I ask you to forgive me for the way I raised my son. I did the best I knew, I tried to do it right, but in some ways I failed. I ask your forgiveness and I ask You to clear away the blockages between my son and me. I desire to see him become the man you created him to be. I ask you to heal the broken places, restore the proper bond between a mother and son, and help me to relate to him as a man. Amen.

*****

Some women may believe that they can organize a Rite of Passage ceremony for their sons and thereby solve the problem. However, creating this momentous occasion goes beyond the repetition of a few words. Other elements are required:

Approval of a boy into manhood by a fraternity of men in his life

Creation of accountability for the heart of a boy to become a man's heart

Responsibility to a company of men to demonstrate manly qualities

Challenge to build the required courage to become a man

This combination of elements is necessary to cultivate a boy's heart for maturity. At the completion of the process, a young man breaks free from boyhood and step into manhood.

I (Henry) was once asked by a pastor's wife how to deal with her 17-year-old son, who was not coming home on time and had begun drinking and smoking. The mother was very worried that her son would also become sexually active and ruin his life. She had given him lecture after lecture without results.

I suggested that she let his father deal with him, and that she should say as little as possible to the young man. If he asked her about anything, she should reply, "Talk to your father about it." The father stepped into his responsibilities and began the instruction and calling-out process of the boy. Within three months, the son casually mentioned to his mother, "I'm not smoking or drinking any more, and the sex thing ... well, that can wait. Dad helped me get my head on straight."

The two most important things a mother can give her son are 'roots' and 'wings.' Roots from the loving nurture of the feminine spirit and the wings to leave to acquire the spirit of manhood.

ACTION STEPS

The following action steps are for men of every age. If you have never participated in a formal Rite of Passage, we strongly suggest that you go through the three steps below. For some men, this will be the confirmation of something that happened to them gradually over a period of years. For others, it will come at a strategic moment to awaken their manhood.

1. Be 'Called Out to Manhood': Read the following aloud; ask God to use your lips to speak this 'call' to your spirit and soul. To plant it deep into your heart, you may want to reread it several times:

   Come out, oh son of the land. Come out, oh son of the land. Come and join the band of men and learn your true heritage. [Say your full name] come join your band of brothers, never to belong again to the world of women and children. Come and receive your manhood ... come be authenticated ... come be validated — cross over to manhood!

2. <u>Take the Oath of Manhood</u>: As before, read aloud but, this time, address yourself to God as you make your vows. If possible, make this pledge in the presence of the men in your life from church or your family. (A word of warning: do not make a vow to God unless you are willing to keep it, see Numbers 30:2 for the consequences):

    I solemnly vow to God and to this band of brothers to walk in manhood and to live by its Code of Honor. I ask each man to hold me accountable to act in a manly way in every area of life: in my devotion to God, in my personal commitments to my family, in my devotion to the body of Christ, and in my relationship to this band of brothers. God, I (full name) *make this fervent commitment with my whole heart.*

3. <u>Receive the Father's Blessing and Answer a Call to Action</u>: We have prayed a blessing over every man who reads this book. Please read aloud the blessing that has been prayed over you:

    I declare that you have been called out into manhood and have been accepted into the company of men. I pray a father's blessing over you that your manhood would be called forth, imparted, and released in you. I pray that authentic manhood will settle upon you. I pray over you the Prayer of Adoption. I ask the Lord to validate you as a man and cause your masculine spirit to grow and to change you. I charge you before God and man to walk in the ways of manhood all the days of your life. I call upon you to duplicate and to multiply this call to manhood in the lives of many young men. Amen.

■■■

Now What?

If you have discovered that, as a man, you fall short in some of the things covered in this book, do not allow yourself to feel discouraged and believe that the changes are too difficult to make. You can do it! And, with God's help, you can make major changes more quickly than you ever thought possible. No one is perfect; we are all in the process of becoming the person God intended.

If you are like most people, you merely read through the Action Steps at the close of each chapter, and then proceeded to the following chapter. The principles in this book really can change your life, but merely *reading* the truth is not enough, *knowing* the truth is necessary to be set free, according to John 8:32. This kind of *knowing* refers to — comprehending, perceiving, understanding, and having a new resolve form in your heart. So you have to *study* the principles found in this book, meditate on them, and allow the Holy Spirit to make them real to you, to receive all its benefits.

For truth to cause change, it must create a new understanding that replaces the lies we have believed and by which we have lived. So, we would suggest that you re-read each chapter at a leisurely pace, make copious notes, underline, or highlight, and take the "Action Steps" seriously by spending at least a week or even a month reading and practicing the suggestions at the end of each chapter. (Some of the Action Steps should actually become a *permanent* part of your routine to create the new lifestyle you desire.)

God created each person to accomplish important things, many of them cannot be achieved until *real* manhood is reached. Regardless of your age or your beginning point, it is never too late to know the satisfaction of being the man God intended … the kind of husband your wife deserves … and the father your children so desperately need.

A Final Word to Women:

No man can be perfect at all times or demonstrate all the aspects of manhood mentioned in this book. Just as you will make mistakes as a wife and mother, even the best-intentioned husband will occasionally blow it. Give him the same grace that you would like to receive.

You cannot make yourself an expert on manhood and teach it to your husband or sons (sorry). The best thing you can do for your husband is encourage him to read this book, and others like it, and to get involved with other Christian men. The most you can do for your 13- to 17-year-old son is suggest that he take his guy-issues to his Dad and spend time bonding with his father.

You cannot fill in the gap an absentee father makes in your son's life, but you can look for a man that God would provide, to be a substitute father to him.

The most powerful things you can do for either your husband or son are: be supportive of their efforts to achieve manhood, be understanding of their failures, and continue to lift them up in your prayers that they will become the men God intended. Most truly successful men have had a praying wife or mother.

Never underestimate the power you have to be a good influence on your husband and children by being the wife and mother to them that God intended.

I (Bart) would like to pray with every woman who wants to be a blessing to the men in her life:

Jesus, I want to be the real woman you intended ... I want to have the relationship with the man you have destined for me ... I want to be a godly influence upon my children. Help me to obtain the extreme success, as a wife, a mother, and in every way You intended for me to be, AMEN.

About Bart Malone

Bart Malone, Pastor of Bridge Christian Fellowship Orlando, came to the Lord at an early age and answered a call to the ministry as a teenager. During his twenties he founded three companies one of which took its first public offering in 1999.

He holds an MBA with a distinction in marketing, has graduated bible school, was ordained to the ministry in 1996 and has served in business and local church ministry for many years.

In addition to local church service, Bart traveled nationally and internationally with John Paul Jackson, founder of Streams Ministries, serving as a son in the faith. Bart also served on staff with Streams Ministries in New Hampshire for eighteen months. Bart, his family, and five other families relocated from the Dallas Forth Worth area to Orlando to plant one of the first Bridge Christian Fellowship churches. In addition to equipping in preaching and teaching, Bart has a ministry of prophecy, dream interpretation, healing, and the release of finances. His heart is to see people reach the purpose for which they were created by God. Bart Malone and his wife Kim have been married for 15 years and have four children Daniel, Austin, Hannah, and Christopher. They live in the Greater Orlando area.

Contact Bart Malone
Senior Pastor, THE BRiDGE ORLANDO
Chairman, Association of Bridge Churches
E:bart@bartmalone.com
273 Bellagio Circle, Sanford Florida 32771

www.BARTMALONE.com

About Dr. Henry Malone

Dr. Henry Malone is president and founder of Vision Life Ministries, a restoration ministry designed to heal the brokenhearted, set at liberty those who are bruised and free those who are captive. Previously a senior pastor for 28 years, he has been ministering translocally to edify and build up the Body of Christ since 1989. Henry emphasizes demonstrating the works of the Kingdom as well as proclaiming the Gospel of the Kingdom. In 1994, he began the Freedom and Fullness Seminars which release the ministry of Jesus in a group setting to bring healing, deliverance and freedom.

Since 1992 he has trained and released interns for deliverance and emotional healing. In 1998 he began the School of Deliverance Ministry to expedite this training. This equipping has expanded into what is now the Personal Development Institute. His desire is to help establish effective balanced deliverance ministries to fulfill the mandate of Luke 4:18. His training emphasizes the important of Christ-like character and a servant's heart as well as the skill and anointing necessary to be vessels of honor in God's kingdom. Affiliated ministries and associate ministers who have been trained through VLM are helping to fulfill this vision throughout the nation. Henry's heart throbs with compassion for the bruised, the broken and the captive—a spirit which he imparts to those whom he trains.

Contact DR. Henry Malone
Senior Minister, Vision Life Ministries
E:info@visionlife.org
P O Box 292455, Lewisville, Texas 75029

www.VISIONLIFE.ORG